Forged in Fire

The Roever Family Story:

A Lifetime of Pain Forged a Lifestyle of Resiliency

Dave Roever

With
Stan Corvin, Jr.
Author of "Vietnam Saga"
(Military Writers Society of America Award Winner)

Forged In Fire
The Roever Family Story:
A Lifetime of Pain Forged a Lifestyle of Resiliency

Dave Roever

Contents

Preface

He heals the brokenhearted and binds up their wounds.
Psalm 147:3

Fifty-three years ago, I was cast into the cruel crucible of war in South Vietnam when a white phosphorus grenade exploded in my hand as I was about to throw it. The blast instantly disfigured my body and forever changed my life. Many of you have seen and heard me speak at church services, school assemblies, and military gatherings. However, until now, none of you know *"The rest of the story."* as a famous Chicago radio commentator would quip in his daily broadcasts.

This book tells of my travels, travails, triumphs, and tragedies as my wife Brenda and I crisscrossed the nation to bring the Gospel of Jesus Christ to the oppressed and brokenhearted. In it, I share my agony of departing Love Field in 1969 and leaving my teenage wife in Texas. Two years later, and terribly disfigured, I'm filled with ecstasy when I walk out of the hospital's burn unit in San Antonio and preach my first sermon.

Oh, my Lord, what a magnificent, exciting journey it has been to serve in God's Kingdom. Although Brenda is no longer with me, having passed away from Covid-19 in February 2021, I feel her presence constantly. Frequently I chuckle, thinking about her firm warning, *"Alright, everyone, keep it together; there are things to be done."* Frankly, I believe she is helping to *"keep it together"* in Heaven while she supports Jesus expanding His Kingdom.

As my earthly ministry winds down, I am eternally grateful for Almighty God's blessings. I look forward to hearing the heavenly words, *"Well done, thou good and faithful servant."* (Matt. 25:21.)

Selah, And Blessings to You All,
Dave Roever

Prologue
Leaving Love - 1969

Holding my wife Brenda a few days after New Year's Day, we stood at the departure gate of Dallas' Love Field. I was preparing to board an American Airlines flight to San Francisco and then a Pan Am Boeing 707 to South Vietnam. I was twenty-one years old; she was nineteen, and I knew I might never kiss her again. So, I pushed her face hard against mine. She was softly crying – her tears were hot and salty, her cheeks feverish and flushed. The lump in my throat cut short my breath, and it hurt to speak. Unaware that in a few months, I would be *"Living in a world of hurt."* I said to Brenda, "Baby, I'll come back home without a scar." Standing there wearing my dress blue uniform, I looked sharp – but she never saw me like that again. Indeed, the man she married, the man she kissed goodbye that day, never returned home.

The Military –
A Call to Duty

*It is said that America without her
soldiers would be like God without His angels.
Yet, I came to realize that some battles will only
be won in the spiritual realm.*

Chapter 1

Alone at Home

Blessed are those who mourn, For they shall be comforted.
Matthew 5:4

On a windy, overcast winter day in early January 2022, I arrived at DFW airport, then drove to my home outside Fort Worth, Texas. Turning onto the rural two-lane black-top road, I soon reached the asphalt drive leading to my house. The gravel crunched under the tires as I slowly stopped the car by the roadside mailbox. Looking at the treelined driveway, I fondly remembered when the four large pine trees growing on the right were tiny seedlings. We planted them when the house was first built five decades earlier. Having gathered the mail, I continued on and parked by the front door. Inside my familiar home, I was met by a profound and unfamiliar silence as I carried my overnight bag inside. After unpacking, I built a fire in the den fireplace. Heavily collapsing into my comfortable leather recliner, I breathed a deep sigh of relief and thought, *"It's so good to be home."*

Gratitude flooded me as I reflected on how God had sent me into His Kingdom for so many years but always brought me back to this perfect safe haven with my loving wife, Brenda. Suddenly I sat up as the reality that she was no longer with me broke my heart one more time.

It was difficult to accept that she had passed away the year before in February. Choking up, I covered my face with both hands and sobbed uncontrollably. Grief-stricken, a deep weariness settled over my body. Her unexpected death from Covid-19 and my constant, unrelenting travel schedule since then were taking a severe physical toll on me. Remembering *Elizabeth Kubler-Ross's* famous list in her classic book,

"On Death and Dying," I thought, *"I don't think I will ever get to the point of acceptance."* She identified that as the final stage of the grieving process.

Recalling *Galatians 6:9* from the New King James Bible, *"And let us not grow weary while doing good, for in due season we shall reap if we do not lose heart."* I was somewhat comforted by the verse, took a deep breath, dried my tears, and relaxed in the recliner. Words that had sustained me in the long-ago years while I was in Brooke Army Medical Center resonated in my thoughts. I had been in excruciating pain, partially submerged underwater in the debridement tank after undergoing the daily torture of peeling away strips of dead skin. Then these words uttered by Rosie helped me to hold on to life. Wearing his faded green scrubs, the massive male nurse was carrying me back to my hospital room when he gently said,

"You'll be fine, big man. You'll see. You'll be fine."

"But Rosie, how can I ever be fine? She's gone now." I tearfully whispered while shaking my head.

"You'll be fine, big man. You'll see. You'll be fine." Then the voice faded away, and I sat alone in the solitude of my den.

Stirred by the strong Texas winds swirling around the house, the burning mesquite and hickory logs sent minute sweet-smelling wisps of smoke into the room. While I watched the flickering flames dance around the logs, memories swirled through my mind – memories of traveling with Brenda and our fifty-three years of marriage and ministry. Memories of the long-sought reaping of the promised harvest, supernatural transformations in new believers, and renewed life revealed as God broke through strongholds and restored shattered dreams in people's hearts. Memories that filled my heart and quickened Holy Spirit within me.

Bowing my head, I prayed aloud, "Dear Lord, little did I know, while serving in the Navy in South Vietnam in 1969, when those devastatingly destructive flames were covering my body, You were preparing a magnificent destiny for me. Worldwide work showing the miraculous power of Your purifying fire as you transformed me, drawing others to You and Your Word and forever strengthening the bond between Brenda and me in our marriage and ministry."

Chapter 2

Saigon - 1969

Have I not commanded you? Be strong and of good courage; do not be afraid, nor be dismayed, for the Lord your God is with you wherever you go. Joshua 1:9

S tepping off the Boeing 707 airplane at Tan Son Nhut airport in Saigon, wearing my dark navy blue dress uniform, I stood on the tarmac watching the helicopters and airplanes flying around the airfield. Immediately I was struck by the warm ninety-degree temperature and humid tropical climate. When I left Dallas Love Field twenty-two hours earlier, it was a cold winter's day, and the temperature was thirty-six degrees with the wind out the north at eighteen miles per hour.

Pulled by a yellow "tug," a dozen luggage carriers hooked together slowly rolled past me, carrying hermetically sealed aluminum caskets containing dead American servicemen. Catching a whiff of something strange, I wondered. *"What is that chemical smell? Can it be formaldehyde embalming fluid preserving their shattered bodies?"* After watching the somber daily news back in the United States and now seeing the nearby caskets, the war suddenly became very real for me. It was especially so after I remembered the number of battle deaths until my arrival today totaled about 40,000 and averaged one American killed in combat every ninety minutes.

Tan Son Nhut International Airport was built in the early 1930s when the French colonial government constructed a small airport with unpaved runways near the village of Tan Son Nhut on the outskirts of Saigon. By mid-1956, a 7,200-foot paved runway had been built. During the Vietnam War, the airbase was a vital facility for the U.S. Air Force and the Republic of Vietnam Air Force. Between 1968 and 1974, it was one of the busiest military bases in the world.

Several blue-painted school buses with thick grenade-proof screens covering the windows pulled up. Once we boarded, they took us to customs, where we exchanged our U.S. dollars for MPC (Military Payment Certificates).

Then we drove into downtown Saigon to a shabby, old French hotel where we stayed for three days of "in-country" orientation. On the first day, we went to the hotel ballroom and received orders for our new duty station assignments. My orders sent me to Riverboat Division 573 at Sa Dec. It was located eighty-eight miles southwest of Saigon on the upper tributary of the My Tho River in the Mekong Delta, where the "Mighty" Mekong River also flowed. The next day we received a series of briefings mainly on surviving noncombat life in Vietnam. Finally, we were assigned our uniforms, gear, and weapons. We would receive no ammunition until we reached our assignment.

Each evening after the orientation classes were over; we were allowed to explore the city which once was known as the "Pearl of the Far East." Saigon's former elegance and beauty as a French colonial capital reminded me of Bourbon Street in New Orleans. The overall atmosphere of deterioration and dilapidation seemed very sad and depressing, at least to me. The narrow streets were littered with trash and packed with small mud-splattered dark blue and canary yellow Fiat cabs, three-wheeled rickshaws locally known as "cyclos," and thousands of bicycles. There also were numerous motorcycles, many driven by young men carrying women sitting behind them tightly clutching their waists with their conical straw "nón là hats hanging down their backs. Most of the women wore traditional white Vietnamese clothing called "ao dais" as the motorcycles weaved in and out of the traffic. Prevalent in the humid air was the pervasive smell of engine exhaust fumes and sidewalk-prepared food dishes containing pungent "nuoc mam," sauce made of decaying fish fermented in brine.

Near the hotel was the infamous avenue, Tu Do Street. It was best known for the darkened and dim "restaurants" and sleazy, American-style bars lit by bright neon signs and filled with deafening rock 'n' roll music. Loudly laughing and "hawking" their wares in very short mini-dresses and sheer blouses, multitudes of young prostitutes called "Saigon tea girls" stood on the wide paved sidewalks outside the establishments. It was as though the Americans were trying to create a back home atmosphere by surrounding themselves with the trappings of Western culture. But, somehow, hometown morality was not present here. Saigon struck me as a city of uncontrolled passions, a place whose moral compass was nonexistent, and indeed a city without the boundaries of human decency.

Arriving downtown on our evening excursions, many guys reached for the girls and prostitutes as soon as they got off the bus. Sickened by what was occurring, I thought, *"What will these guys be like when this thing is over? Whatever they may have done at home, God knows what they will do here."*

STREETS OF SAIGON

Chapter 3

Sa Dec PBR Base

Though I walk in the midst of trouble, You will revive me;
You will stretch out Your hand Against the wrath of my enemies, and Your right
hand will save me. Psalm 138:7

O n the fourth day, I left Tan Son Nhut Air Base aboard a twin-engine C-123 troop carrier and landed at Can Tho. Then I boarded an OH-58 Bell Jet Ranger helicopter, which, after a 45-minute flight, took me to my base at Sa Dec. Arriving at the Patrol Boat Base (PBR), I was met by two officers who warmly greeted me then we drove to their headquarters in a jeep.

The small compound housed about one-hundred-fifty personnel for the PBR boat base and the SEAL team. The boats were docked on the river about a half mile outside the perimeter, and I thought Sa Dec was a sharp little compound. I was issued sheets, pillowcases, and blankets and assigned a bunk in the enlisted barracks. Ammunition for my M-16 was issued from the boats. I carried six or eight magazines, each with twenty rounds, and at first, I slept with that gun.

When I walked into my new living quarters, I was surprised to see some guys had their own little homemade concession stands. They were real entrepreneurs selling booze, electronic gadgetry, and trinkets that passed as local art. Each bunk had a personality all its own. The guys made them homey by putting up pictures and posters, photos of their family or the girl back home. I remember seeing a lot of Rolling Stones, Beatles, and peace symbol posters.

I never put up any posters; the only personal touch was one picture of Brenda. I carried no pictures on my person either. I even took off my wedding ring and carefully stored it along with other valuables in the toe of one of my old boots. If I were captured, the enemy would try to use knowledge about my family to manipulate me.

That first day, I was introduced to my commanding officer and team. There were eight of us, four crew members on each of two boats that always patrolled together. My CO was Lieutenant Rambo. (His name is no joke. I suppose Sylvester Stallone's Rambo is pure coincidence.) He was probably thirty-five years old and as gutsy as they come. Rambo was an outstanding man, very capable and responsible.

After moving my things in, we went down to see the boats. I could hardly wait to get on board because that was what I was there to do — to get on that boat! Each eight-man group was transported to the dock area in the back of a large "deuce-and-a-half" U.S. Navy truck with big knobby tread tires. Docked on the river were our boats and the flat cargo barges where supplies and ammunition were warehoused. Ten patrol boats were docked there, two for each crew team. There were no names on the boats, no numbers or identification. That prevented the Viet Cong from taking revenge on any particular boat.

The next morning, I started going out on patrol with my two-boat eight-man team. I remember inspecting some civilian boats on my first day out, learning the ropes. We inspected boats every day unless we knew we were going in to provoke a firefight with the enemy. The Vietnamese river craft we searched were mostly old wooden vessels ranging in size from small sampans to huge multicarrier junks as big as small tankers. Searching one of those large junks often was an all-day job. Anytime we saw a watercraft looking suspicious, we stopped and searched it. There were a million places on those vessels to hide stuff. We had to look behind everything, never knowing when we would reach into something and have our heads blown off. It was scary, especially poking inside a dark, cramped cargo hold.

We looked for hidden passages or doors that wouldn't open on the big tankers. We had to poke long poles down through holds filled with rice, feeling for anything solid that would indicate weapons or ammunition caches. Our biggest problem was searching the water taxis: many were twenty or forty feet long and carried dozens of people. The Viet Cong blended in with the crowd and could easily pull out a knife and stab you. A long M-16 rifle was no protection at all. So, I developed a modified weapon just for such situations. I took a .30 caliber M-1 carbine, formed a pistol grip by cutting its stock off, and cut the front barrel off just in front of the receiver slide. I taped three banana clip magazines together, each containing thirty rounds to form my front-hand grip. When finished, I had a highly maneuverable fully-automatic weapon no more than ten inches in length.

A few days after arriving, I was part of a big armada, sixteen boats if I recall correctly. The mission was to take over a place we nicknamed the Devil's Hole. It was an island crisscrossed by man-made canals with a village full of Viet Cong. Although I was a rookie, I was the front gunner in the lead boat and the first man to enter the Devil's Hole area of operations (AO). Our commanding officer warned us to expect heavy resistance. The plan, he explained, was to try to pull the Viet Cong into a confrontation so we could let them see what they were up against. It was no secret ambush operation. We knew they were there, and they knew we were coming.

The VC immediately began firing at us once we arrived at the island with the sixteen boats' twin diesel engines roaring. The river bank seemed to explode towards us as their tracers flashed at our boats. The enemy relied on the usual AK-47 machine guns, plus a few rocket-propelled grenades and B-40 rockets. We were the ones with the heavy artillery, and we pounded them mercilessly until our ammunition was almost exhausted. When we finished our attack, no enemy was firing; and anyone alive had retreated. In a firefight like that, you don't see people, you just see the tracer bullets from their automatic weapons, and you fire back at the source of the tracer.

Beaching our boats on the grassy riverbank, we flushed out the bunkers, captured some VC prisoners, and began the body count. Seeing the bodies always made me sick at heart. Several questions always haunted me; *"Did I kill that guy in the bunker? Did I kill any of the dead?"* We left the bodies on the blood-stained ground and took our prisoners back to the base in our boats. After receiving medical attention, they were sent to the South Vietnamese forces for interrogation. Many times, the prisoners were killed after they were tortured and questioned. Their bodies were dumped in the river.

The conflicting emotions of being involved in the intense firefight were draining. I felt elated that I was still alive and sick at the sight of the casualties. It all seemed like a game to some GIs who would take trophies. They wanted to cut off the ears of the enemy dead, that sort of thing. There was more restraint if we were in a large group. However, anything was possible in a small group, such as our team of eight men.

When we returned to the barracks after the raid on Devil's Hole, most of the guys went straight to the bar and got drunk. That behavior was a standard operating procedure for many of them. My values did not allow me the luxury of anesthetizing the pain with alcohol. I went straight to my bunk, put my face in my pillow, and cried, saying, *"For God and country, for God and country, for God and country."* That was the last time I cried, however, because I, too, became callous.

SA DEC BASE 1967

Chapter 4

Brenda's Care Packages

She does him good and not evil all the days of her life.
Proverbs 31:12

I didn't need alcohol to take away the pain of events like the firefight at Devil's Hole. I had a more effective pain-killer for the desperate fear and loneliness of war: Brenda's letters, tape-recorded messages, and packages she sent stuffed with goodies arrived twice a month. I virtually had an addiction to Fritos and bean dip, and she always included these in the treasure trove packed in the middle of the "care" packages. She also sent candy bars, gum, and cookies. The fragile items were protected with large bags of popcorn used as packing material. My buddies went after the popcorn; an unwritten law about treats from home required that everyone shared something; you shared or suffered being an outcast or worse. Anyway, I was always left with the best of the provisions and tore into them for the sweetness it gave, the taste of Brenda's kindness.

The tape-recorded messages arrived more often, about once weekly. At first, I had a little reel-to-reel recorder, but the power in Vietnam was different and distorted the speed and sound. We soon had cassette players, which improved the quality of the tapes. You can't imagine how hearing Brenda's voice while sitting in the jungle made her seem much closer to me. I would sit down and listen to the tape in the barracks through earphones if others were around, but I preferred the tone of the regular speaker.

I always listened and responded to her immediately, finding somewhere to be alone. Sometimes I talked to her as if we were lying in bed together, pretending that it had been a normal, long, hard day, and now we were lying there in the dark, speaking openly and without urgency as couples who cherish the last minutes together before dropping off to sleep. Then I often reminisced about our days together. I always ended my messages to Brenda by contemplating returning from Vietnam and being alone with her in our own home. That fantasy and those weekly tapes kept the closeness of our relationship very much alive. Regularly hearing Brenda's voice helped bring sanity to the seemingly insane world I was living in.

I never talked about the details of the war. Brenda knew enough to realize the danger I was in without my driving her crazy with frightening details. I wanted to share these things with the one I loved, but that abiding love prevented me from it. She wrote to me every night before she went to bed, scenting her letters with Chanel No. 5® perfume.

She worked at Sears Roebuck & Co. and lived with her parents. That setting provided the context for her simple letters. She told me every minute detail of her day, the chicken she had prepared for dinner, her new blouse, and a movie she had attended. I was always delighted to receive her letters. They all began in the same way, "I love you, I miss you, I want you." The last statement meant the most to me. If she didn't still want me, she could hardly love me with the strength necessary for her to remain faithful. A beautiful woman her age would have opportunities to cheat, but repetition of those lines made me sense the strength of her loyalty.

There were times when the loneliness of the war was so bad that I might have deserted if given half a chance – but how do you hitchhike out of a jungle to San Diego? I'm saying that without her letters, I believe I truly would have gone crazy.

However, fantasy and imagination can be powerful defenses when used right. I would take every detail in those letters and mentally use them to transport myself back home. I sat at the table where they ate the meal Brenda had prepared; I drove with her to work. I attended church and Sunday school with her. Her letters filled me with enthusiasm for living again because they allowed me to block out the war and pour myself into all those things which make life worthwhile.

Later Brenda told me that my letters always made her cry, reminding her how precarious our future life had become. I may also have reacted that way, except my memories about home were so intense that I was there for hours in my daydreams. The war became an unreal thing. Those letters, tapes, and packages kept me going; I wouldn't have been able to bear the war without them.

About three months into my tour of duty, I found out the date of my first R&R. It was to take place five days after our anniversary. I collected all the brochures I could find and decided on Hawaii. Brenda was so excited that she started packing that same day. From then on, we had an extra hedge of protection against the difficulties of the war; we could tell ourselves, "Well, four months (three, two, and so on), then we will be together again."

We started to allow ourselves to look to the future in other ways. We had decided not to conceive a child while I was in training, but now that I was in Vietnam, we started discussing names for our future babies. We also considered what port assignments I should put in for after completing my tour in Vietnam – I would have two more years left to serve once I left combat behind. It was my love for Brenda that sustained me in Vietnam. Without her, I'm not sure I would have been able to bear the loneliness and horror of war.

Chapter 5

Tan An PBR Base

The Lord will cause your enemies who rise against you to be defeated before your face; they Shall come out against you one way and flee before you seven ways.
Deuteronomy 28:7

When we received orders to move from Sa Dec to Tan An, we were told we were relieving a company with a 90% casualty rate. At least that was the "scuttlebutt" going around. At the time, I thought, *"This is it; this is where Vietnam gets me. It's going to kill me, and I'll die here."* I became very depressed, thinking that I might die. What bothered me about death more than anything else was losing Brenda. I just couldn't face the thought that I wouldn't be able to hold her again. I wasn't focused on physical suffering and death. The one thing I was afraid of was not finishing my life with Brenda. To me, death meant the loss of the future with her.

The depression prompted by the move to Tan An lasted about a week. Finally, I contemplated ending it all as I thought, *"I can't go on like this."* That afternoon, we received a batch of mail containing a letter for me that brought a powerful message. Miraculously there was a letter from Reverend E. R. Anderson telling me that The North Texas District Council of the Assemblies of God church was granting me a license to preach by proxy. That broke the depression more than anything else. I had a card that said I was still in the fellowship with those home brethren. On the day I was saying, *"I'm giving up,"* God said, *"Hey, I'm promoting you. What are you giving up for?"*

I felt like I had just been slapped in the face by a loving father. I believe He probably smiled and said, *"You'll get over it. I don't like what you did, but I forgive you; now get on with your life. Remember, my grace is sufficient for you because my grace is perfected in your weakness."* God was taking the opportunity to show me my complete dependency on Christ, to let me see that I should not trust in my own personal righteousness. I needed to depend on the Lord. From that moment on, I started to leave behind an Old Testament faith focused on models of Samson and the prophets. I began to look more directly at the Master. All Old Testament heroes were manifestations of Him. Christ alone embodied the collective experience of those who had foreshadowed Him. The Lord certainly never let me question his grace. The letter from Reverend Anderson was God's grace to me at the exact time when I needed it. God was saying, *"Davey, I love you. All the self-doubt and recrimination are behind you."*

The Tan An compound was located west of Saigon. The Mekong River splits into two tributaries there. The major branch is called the Vam Co, which splits into small offshoots called the Vam Co Tay and the Vam Co Dong. Sa Dec was on the Mekong, and Tan An was on the Vam Co Tay. We were close to Cambodia the whole time, which accounts for the dangerous nature of our duties because the North Vietnamese infiltrated South Vietnam through Cambodia.

The north-south Cambodian border curves to Saigon in a parrot's beak shape. It was extremely dangerous territory because the enemy could keep men and supplies in the neutral territory within striking distance of Saigon. American troops weren't yet permitted into Cambodia, so the mission of the navy's riverboat patrols was to prevent the VC movement of arms, ammunition, and personnel from Cambodia into the area around Saigon.

Once the bombing of the Ho Chi Minh Trail ended, the enemy flooded down that trail through Laos and Cambodia directly into the parrot's beak. We had proof that the bombing of the Ho Chi Minh Trail was effective because when it stopped, the North Vietnamese Army rushed through. All we had were a few little fiberglass boats to use to fight against the North Vietnamese forces. Many people back home saw the Americans as big strong men fighting puny little Viet Cong teenagers. But the reality was that we were up against a major enemy force well-armed with plenty of weapons and resources.

Tan An was a small village of about three thousand people, with a large U.S. Army base across town from our compound situated on the river. Our barracks was a floating barge called a mobile base two (MB2). It was a big flat barge with a superstructure built on it like a ship's quarters with hatches between rooms. Our rooms were airconditioned, extremely modern, well-lit, and hospital-clean. About one hundred guys were quartered in an MB2, in bunks stacked three high but laid out at different heights so you couldn't just look from one side of the barracks to the other. Under each bunk mattress was a storage compartment about six inches deep, the width and length of the entire bed. Additional locker units were positioned nearby.

Our boats were tied up alongside the barge, which was not secure. Because there were no guards or American security forces up or downstream, we kept a guard posted to watch for anything floating down the river. Water mines were a constant concern, so when the guards saw anything troublesome, they would set off concussion grenades. That meant that occasionally we would be startled by a loud explosion in the water.

Every aspect of our life was more tense and stressful at Tan An than at Sa Dec. We had no regular daily schedule but would go out on long patrols, often on consecutive nights. As enemy action picked up, our interactions with one another got tenser. It was obvious the guys were getting on each other's nerves.

I had no opportunity to hold modest church services at Tan An. For one thing, my guitar and microphone had to stay at Sa Dec. I did have an old Stella guitar, and I would sit around and pick that guitar and sing for my enjoyment and musical improvement, but I could never get a group of guys together. I couldn't even get into a daily schedule of private devotions because our routine didn't permit anything to be done regularly. We had to be ready at any time to jump into action. Sometimes I would pray at my bunk, but I would almost always be harassed. If I read my Bible, I was asking for trouble. Some guy would walk by and try to flip it shut, saying something like, "You @#$%&! preacher!" I finally decided that maintaining peace with my teammates was more important than making a big deal out of my devotional life, so I stopped praying in public.

I got the nickname "Preacher Man" after moving to Tan An. When our bunk assignments were made, I ended up with a couple of guys close by who were a pain to be around. The guy who bunked above me became my chief antagonist. He and two other guys came up with my nicknames, "Preacher Man," "Dudley Do-right," and "Doctor Dolittle." I gave them nicknames of my own: "Pervert Number One," "Pervert Number Two," and "Pervert Number Three." These nicknames, on both sides, weren't truly malicious; they could be used in a friendly or stinging way, depending on the context. Pervert Number One was a big stocky fellow with dark hair, a roundish face, and a captivating smile on the rare occasions when he smiled. He was a smart, scheming guy who was occasionally outright mean. He could make you feel like the loneliest nerd on God's earth with one tongue lashing. He also slyly manipulated the other guys to reinforce his opinion. A natural leader, he could make anyone an outcast.

In my locker, I kept civilian clothes, some nice shoes, sports shirts, and dress slacks and wore them when I wasn't on patrol. I was the only guy who wore decent clothes when he wanted to relax. The guys would mock me because they knew that caring about my appearance helped improve my morale. Dressing like that reminded me that God has conferred on man a dignity greatly superior to his other earthly creations. Pervert Number One, smart as he was, saw the meaning of these manners and was especially irritated by them.

Sometimes when my teammates were preparing to go out and have a night on the town, they would say something like, "Come on, Preacher Man. You come with us." Other times they brought one or two prostitutes into the barracks and passed them around. Of course, that was strictly forbidden, but they did it anyway. I walked out; keeping away from these scenes was the only thing I could do. I escaped to a quiet corner of the barracks to dwell on memories of Brenda and listen to cassette tapes of her voice – which always renewed my spirit and strengthened my conscience.

Alcohol and sex were prevalent, but I never saw any drug use among the guys around me. The evidence is clear that some GIs used heroin, hashish, and pot in Vietnam. I'm sure the main reason why none of our guys got into drugs was that we were doing such dangerous work in small, close-knit teams. If anybody had been high, we wouldn't have trusted him. He would have put the rest of us in danger of being killed. It was almost an unwritten rule: anybody using dope would be terminated by his comrades. Too much was at stake.

During my time at Tan An, enemy activity steadily increased. We encountered more frequent sniper fire and ambushes. Sa Dec was R&R compared to Tan An. As I've indicated, we were on twenty-four-hour calls without regular shifts. We had only a few hours to relax between shifts, which ran as long as sixteen or eighteen hours. Still, the commanding officers tried not to work us until fatigue produced careless attitudes that could prove deadly. It was essential to remain alert.

We did our job well and shut down the rivers to the communists. They frequently ambushed us, trying to scare us off, but it didn't work. We kept coming back, and they never gained control of the rivers. They had the manpower, but we had superior firepower and much better equipment to move it around. All they had were battered old sampans which they used to ambush and attack us by employing hit-and-run tactics.

Our patrols were largely sent out in response to intelligence information about the enemy's activity. The reconnaissance planes took infrared photographs at night and used a form of thermal imaging radar that was sensitive to temperatures. It could pick up the collective body heat of enemy troops. Helicopters frequently reported information about the enemy activity, and small two-seat L-19 model Cessna 170 spotter planes called "Bird Dogs" also reported on enemy movements. We generally had reliable information, so we knew when and where to go. However: our best source of information was often the "Chou Hoi," who was a surrendering Viet Cong soldier. They would often tell us what was about to happen instead of what had already occurred.

One time, for instance, aerial photography spotted a Viet Cong R&R encampment across the Cambodian border. I volunteered to go with the unit sniper and Lieutenant Rambo on a special mission to check them out. We took a little fiberglass boat powered by two small but strong Johnson outboard motors. I carried an M-60 machine gun (the same gun that Sylvester Stallone's Rambo used in the movie), the sniper carried his Remington Model 40 scoped sniper rifle in .308

caliber, and Lieutenant Rambo carried the most unusual weapon I ever saw in Vietnam, a fully automatic, sawed-off 12-gauge shotgun: one bad weapon.

We cautiously made our way up some small shallow man-made canals, crossing the border into Cambodia as we did. Rounding a curve in a narrow canal, we surprised fifty to one hundred stark-naked Viet Cong bathing in the canal. Remarkably a large R&R center was there. The enemy's weapons were stacked in a big pile in the clearing on the bank. All of their flip-flop shoes were lined up along the river. Their clothes were piled together, and they had a stack of little bamboo cages containing snakes they had caught and planned to eat later. The stunned look on their faces when they saw us coming was indescribable. We were as surprised as they were, and I knew we were in a predicament about what to do. Having crossed the Cambodian border, we didn't want an international incident, so I started firing machine gun bursts above their heads. They scattered in every direction, naked as jaybirds. One even swam across the canal and ran off on the other side. None of them had weapons, and they knew my aim would suddenly improve if they went near them. They must have praised Buddha that we didn't kill them because everything happened in seconds.

We beached the boat and searched the camp to determine how much equipment and supplies were coming in and by whom. In empty mortar cans, we found large supplies of granular carbide, which they used in lanterns to provide light at night. We burned their clothes and shoes, destroyed their food, and released the caged snakes. We destroyed their weapons with a plastic explosive called C-4. That incident was more comical than anything else, although returning through the narrow canals was very scary. This enemy encounter happened about three weeks before I was injured.

Our job was to patrol the Vam Co Tay River. One section made an S-curve, eliminating one of the loops. It was an area with a heavy amount of communist activity. Because of the terrain, nobody had controlled what the VC did there for a long time. We had to clear the canal because nobody wanted to go through it. It was narrow and shallow, and the boat occasionally scraped the bottom. One night, because of the poor navigation skills of a substitute coxswain, we ran aground at low tide and were stuck like sitting ducks for twelve hours until the tide came back in.

Another day when we patrolled the canal, I had a strong sense of the enemy's presence. All the signs were there. We could see where they beached their sampans and crossed the canal. Everything was quiet. I decided to clean the guns and test them more out of boredom than anything else. Using the radio, I called headquarters to get clearance. Standing orders required getting permission from headquarters to fire weapons if we weren't being fired upon. When friendly villages were nearby, we had to get clearance to return fire even if we were being fired upon, which was a crazy rule of engagement. (ROE)

Permission was granted for us to H&I – "harass and interdict." I adjusted my sights on a field about five hundred yards away. I aimed at a large white tomb topped by a cross. Like many Christian objects and buildings, it was left over from the French colonial period. I thought I would take a single shot with one of my front .50 caliber guns and see where the tracer would go. I put in tracers and squeezed off one round. "Bam!" I missed it a hundred yards to the right. I moved the front sight of the gun toward the other gun and tried again. "Bam!" I missed it again, but this time I was closer. I shot several more times. Finally, I gave up adjusting the aim of single shots. As we did in a firefight, I decided to walk the bullets onto the target. So, I connected the second gun, pushed the firing button on the electronic firing mechanism, and started shooting. I had it on the tomb in a second or two. I could see tracers ricocheting and concrete dust flying everywhere. Eventually, I aimed for the cross and blew it off, with the whole top of the tomb sliding behind it.

We didn't know it, but there was an Army L-19 Cessna 170 "Bird Dog" flying high above us. I was firing, and he didn't know what was happening. He tried calling us on our radio but wasn't on the same frequency. Finally, he picked us up and started screaming, "Stop firing, stop firing. What's wrong? Are you in a firefight? Where's the enemy? I'll help you."

I felt like a jerk, but I didn't know he was there, and he should have contacted us. I said, "I'm sorry, man, we had no idea you were up there.

No one told us." I told him we had clearance, and I was doing some H&I firing.

"What are you hitting?" he asked.

I mentioned the old tomb and told him where it was so he could check it out. He flew over the tomb site, and a couple of seconds later, he called on the radio, yelling his head off. "You won't believe what I'm seeing. That's no tomb; that's an arsenal – full of guns and ammunition."

He radioed for a backup team, and we stayed on location because we thought the enemy knew what we had done. The Army pilot flew a team in to check it out and found a huge cache of supplies and equipment. I received a medal from the Vietnamese Army for discovering the enemy cache – purely by accident.

We learned something important about the enemy that day: They used our respect for the dead to bury arms and ammunition in tombs. We weren't graverobbers, and they knew we usually respected burial sites. Looking back on that incident, I'm now aware of my callous actions, notwithstanding the beneficial results. We discovered they used many tombs in that area where they would sleep or hide during the day before moving on at night. We learned they had fabricated fake cardboard tombs, which they folded and carried with them at night. Then during the day, they set them up and slept in them. They stayed far enough away so their tombs looked real, but they slept almost under our noses.

I wondered if the South Vietnamese would be able to make a democratic form of government work if they had the chance. Honestly, I didn't think much about these larger political questions during daily survival and doing my job. I just hoped that if these people could ever be free long enough, they would work out their problems. I hoped that a basic sense of morality would evolve. Yet, in my heart, I couldn't imagine how that would happen without the values of the Christian faith. That's why in 1974 and 1975, I went back to Vietnam as a missionary evangelist. I wanted to see truth and righteousness come to Vietnam, not just democracy. I believe if you can get the gospel preached in a country, it has a way of straightening the place out.

I don't know how democracy can flourish when greed and evil go unchecked. Democracy requires self-restraint, which a sinful culture generally doesn't exhibit. That's why our job in South Vietnam was so difficult, if not impossible. At home in America, many people marched to sympathize with the Viet Cong instead of praying for us. This added to our difficulties and had a detrimental effect on military morale.

Americans at home were often the unsuspecting victims of what I know from firsthand experience to be communist propaganda. The Viet Cong tried to create situations in which Americans were blamed for destroying the country they were attempting to save. They frequently set up ambushes at sites between the American forces and a vulnerable village. They planned to open fire on us, hoping we would lack restraint and start indiscriminately firing back, killing more civilians than enemy troops. Then they'd take photos and videos of it, put them in newspapers, and tell the world what bad boys we were. That was a strategy we had to guard against. At all times, we had to know where we were and where the villages were located.

The Viet Cong knew that the indiscriminate killing of innocent people was unacceptable to Americans. I agree and would rather the enemy go unpunished than destroy the innocent. I can tell you the teams I was associated with did their best to protect the civilians.

The Viet Cong fought that war using such tactics. They knew that we would not do anything to destroy innocent people because they lived among the civilians. They used the babies, mothers, wives, and older people to hide behind. The communists literally hid behind the women's skirts in that war. These are still the basic tactics of terrorist warfare worldwide. The same methods evildoers have used for eons.

Chapter 6

Mop Det - Buồn

(English: Fatso – Sad)

To everything there is a season, A time for every purpose under heaven A time to kill, And a time to heal; A time to break down, And a time to build up; A time to weep, And a time to laugh; Ecclesiastes 3:1,3,4

Not long before my injury, I began receiving training to be the next captain. Therefore, I was occasionally given command of the boat. One night, I was studying the radar when I noticed a vegetation gap on the riverbank I had never noticed before. It wasn't on the map either. The next day, we went up the river to find it. It wasn't there, and I became even more curious about the gap.

After carefully searching, I discovered a little man-made canal off the main river we had never inspected. It had been well concealed by using the overhanging brush at the entrance. The Viet Cong would pull the brush back at night and go up the narrow canal to a small village. The canal was so shallow that we had to wait until the water level rose. We wanted to ensure we did not scrape the bottom or get trapped in the canal. Fortunately, the tide was coming in, and navigation became easier. The canal ended in a cul-de-sac at the village of Thu Thua, which seemed to have escaped the ravages of war. The canal was narrow, so I made sure we maneuvered the boats around to be in position for a quick getaway if necessary. Then I beached my boat on the bank and leaped off the bow onto a rickety little pier.

I saw children everywhere while I was walking through the village. There were so many that I wondered if Thu Thua was an oasis amid the desert of war, a place where people brought their children to keep them safe. True or not, there were many women and children in this village and very few men, except ancient "Papasans." I walked past a little hut where an old fellow sat out front, engraving Buddhist coffins. We also saw a warehouse storing big blocks of ice insulated completely with rice hulls hauled in from Saigon.

The kids wouldn't come near me. They stayed back just beyond the reach of my gun butt and looked as if they were afraid I would hit them. I was surprised by their obvious fear because I thought they must have been some of the same kids who had fearlessly approached us down the river. I was making inroads with some of them and had begun to make friends.

When our boats came by, those little kids would paddle out in their tiny sampans, hold out their hands, and say, "GI, you give me chop, chop." They wanted food. I loved seeing the children, but I was always nervous with them around the boat because of the potential for an accident.

I remember one day when a kid returned after I had told him to beat it. He was alone in his little boat and sat on the bow. "Chop, chop, GI, you give me chop, chop." He was persistent, and I couldn't ignore him because he was such a cute little guy.

I motioned for him to come alongside, then I reached down to help pull him up into the boat, but he must have thought I would hit him. These kids were skittish, and I couldn't blame them. When he leaned back, he fell off the padded rag where he was sitting. That's when I noticed he didn't have any legs. I thought he had been sitting cross-legged. In Vietnamese, I asked him what had happened. He told me he had stepped on a booby trap. He said that word in English. I pulled the kid up in the boat and held him in my lap. Let me tell you; I was fighting back the tears; it's one thing to see the enemy or even civilians dead. The dead aren't in pain. It's another thing to see people suffering, especially innocent children.

I held this poor child up against me and started scrounging for food. I found one of the cornflake candy bars that came from the combat rationing package. We never ate them; we just threw them under the engine cover in the bilge. The cellophane wrapper was all greasy, but the inside was clean, so I opened it and gave it to the kid. You could see he was in heaven, eating that old candy bar.

While he was eating, I noticed that his thumb had been smashed. He told me that he had learned to walk on his hands and that someone had stepped on his thumb. I could see that his thumbnail had separated and was hanging on by a thread of connective tissue. It must have caused much pain, or he would have pulled it off. I could see bloody pus oozing from under the cuticle and running down his arm as he ate.

The kid was going to get gangrene, and I thought, "*Lord, he's lost his legs, and now he's going to lose his arm, maybe his life.*"

I sat him up on the engine cover, propped him against the gunwale, and started rummaging through the first-aid kit while he ate his candy bar. I washed his hands and then poured Mercurochrome all over his thumb. By then, the kid trusted me. I pulled off the loose thumbnail like you might pull out a child's baby tooth, and despite the pain, he just kept eating. Then I began squeezing out the bloody pus, about gagging myself and still fighting off tears. He looked at me, ate more of the candy bar, and looked again. Sometimes he winced a little from the pain. The more I squeezed, the more stuff came out until I felt I'd have to squeeze his whole arm to clean the wound.

The little fellow's thumb was finally cleaned, and I covered it with a huge gauze bandage. I ended up taping his whole hand to keep it clean. He started waving his hand at the kids on the bank. They were all envious because he had received something they had not. I set him back in his boat, said goodbye, and he paddled away. I noted our coordinates and later called in a medical operations team to go in there and help the kid.

Not long afterward, I met the kid in more pleasant circumstances caused by my foolishness. One day, I was bored on the boat, so I decided to detonate an explosive satchel charge underwater. Pulling the delayed fuse, I tossed the thing overboard but got scared when it didn't sink. Instead of sinking the twenty feet I had anticipated, it was only five inches below the surface when it detonated. The explosion lifted the back of the boat out of the water and spun us completely around. I almost blew us out of the water. We began laughing and screaming.

Then a miracle happened. I call it that because it reminds me of one of Jesus' miracles. The charge must have landed on top of a school of fish because thousands, literally thousands, of fish immediately floated to the surface, belly up. Some were dead, but many of the fish were stunned. The children on the bank of the river saw what had happened. They jumped into their little boats, and a flotilla of children came paddling out there and started scooping up fish by the hundreds. They loaded their boats until I thought they would sink. The boy with no legs was among them, shouting, "GI, you number one! GI, you number one!" He loved me.

A couple of days after I blew up the fish for everyone, we went up the canal to Thu Thua, where I assumed some of the same kids lived. That's why I was surprised they were so skittish. Of course, I had caught everyone off guard. They weren't expecting anybody, much less two loud boats. Seeing their fear, I returned to my boat and took off my weapons and ammunition belt. When I returned to the village, the kids came up to me.

One kid, only about five or six years old, walked up to me, touched my hand, and then jumped back to see if I would hit him. He came back a second time and touched me, then jumped back out of the way again. The third time I saw him coming, I thought, "*I will have fun with this little guy.*"

When he reached out to touch my hand, I grabbed his. His eyes rolled up in their sockets, and he let out a wail of terror as though I would skin him alive. I gathered him up, pulled him in tight, and held his little tummy up against my chest, trying to get him to quit kicking and screaming. Gradually, the screaming subsided, and I could feel his body relax. Finally, he looked up at me and said, "GI, you number one."

When that little fellow relaxed, all the other kids just stormed me. They crawled up my legs, hung onto my arms, and clambered up my back. One of them tried to climb from my shoulders to the top of my head. I tried to shuffle along with them on me but finally collapsed under their weight. They were laughing, and I was laughing. It felt so good to make children laugh instead of making widows cry over their dead husbands and orphaned babies.

The kids started chanting, "Mop Det! Mop Det! Mop Det!" I continued to play with them, wrestling with them on the ground.

The sound of the children's happy voices came to me like the breath of God, scraping away my callousness with the sandpaper of love. I wanted to cry. The only softening tears are those that come from joy, not anger. The tears I'd shed from causing pain had only hardened me, like water added to the heavy powder of concrete.

When I was ready to leave, the kids said, "You okay, GI. You number one Mop Det. You come back. You come back tomorrow."

They could speak a little broken English, as could most people in Vietnam. It troubled me that they could speak broken English yet act like we were the first Americans they'd ever seen. As dirty as a pig from rolling in the dirt, I returned to the boat and told the guys, "We're coming back here tomorrow."

They said, "No way. They'll kill us, man; they'll set an ambush."

"How do the VC know we are coming back tomorrow? I didn't tell them we were. I just told the kids." I said.

"That's all it takes."

"We're taking our chances. We're coming back. We can do more to win this war by making friends than killing enemies."

The next day, we went back. It was my command decision. As we turned up the little canal, we spotted the same guy I had held in my arms. He was waiting there, almost as though he had been appointed to keep watch. Our boats were unmarked, so he looked everybody over. I was standing up on the bow like Captain Hook.

When we started up the canal, the kid ran as fast as he could, screaming at the top of his lungs, "Mop Det! Mop Det! Mop Det!"

Soon all the kids started running out into the clearing. They nearly swamped the boat at the dock. I stepped off, again without weapons of any kind, and walked into the village. I swear I emptied the huts of that village of every kid. Mothers came out to watch in obvious amazement as the kids flocked to me. I felt like the Pied Piper of Thu Thua.

I played with the children again that day. I didn't have any treats, but I took popcorn when we returned on the third day. I had recently received a package from Brenda with a big plastic bag of popcorn stuffed around the contents. When I arrived with that popcorn, a sea of kids jumped up and down, chanting, "Mop Det! Mop Det! Mop Det!"

It was a little bit of heaven. They mobbed me again and went wild over the food. The mothers loved it; they loved to see their children love me. That was the day I found out what Mop Det meant: Fatso!

I knew that we would have to quit soon. The VC would find out and take advantage of our lowered guard to ambush us. But we returned to the village on the fourth day.

As we drew near the canal, I saw smoke drifting up over the trees coming from the direction of the village. When we arrived at the mouth of the canal, we saw the Viet Cong had moved in and were destroying the place, burning the rice fields and hooches and asserting their authority by taking over the village of women and kids. My heart pounded with fear. I just prayed the children were safe.

The U.S. military was already working to stop the Viet Cong raid. As we were getting ready to go up the canal, we saw American helicopters flying overhead and American tanks coming through the brush. We heard machine-gun fire coming from the village area. Since the Americans had not yet arrived, it could only be from communist troops.

The communists tried to escape, but they weren't fast enough. Our tanks caught them, and I watched the village being wiped out. The tanks drove on top of big bunkers full of VC and crushed them. When the tanks finished their job, we went in behind them to check out the village. We saw the dead children gunned down not by tank shells or helicopter rockets but by Viet Cong machine guns. When they knew the American troops were coming in, the VC turned around and slaughtered the women and children, making it look like the Americans were responsible for their deaths. They killed those little kids who had been crawling all over me and eating popcorn the day before.

Sick at heart, we turned the boats around and came back out. From the boat, my team could follow the movement of what was left of the enemy, so I got on the radio, ordered an air strike, called in the coordinates, and then watched a jet drop bomb after bomb on what was left of Thu Thua. The concussion ring hit me when the first bombs detonated, knocked me down onto the boat, and whipped-lashed the antennas. The force was strong enough to hurt some of my internal organs.

That day I lost my hope and passion for coming out of the war alive. I wouldn't take my own life, but I volunteered for every deadly mission. I was seeking Viet Cong suicide. I felt responsible for those children's deaths and the village's destruction. It was the most horrible day of my life. This was a terrible irony; trying to be friendly, I had placed the women and children in grave jeopardy. And I, the Pied Piper of Thu Thua, was responsible for the enemy incinerating those children's corpses and eradicating the last vestiges of that village's existence. I didn't speak as we went back to the base. I also didn't cry or shed any tears.

Translated into English, Thu Thua means "lose, lose." It was a place where all involved did indeed lose. They lost innocent people, the way of life in that small village, and the future of what might have been for them all. I lost the vision that men can overcome evil simply by doing good. I learned close up and far too personally that *"We do not wrestle against flesh and blood, but against principalities, against powers, against the rulers of the darkness of this age, against spiritual hosts of wickedness in the heavenly places."* It has been said that America without her soldiers would be like God without His angels. Yet, I came to realize that some battles will only be won in the spiritual realm. As Paul described in Ephesians chapter 6, there is a bigger battle being fought than we can comprehend on this side of heaven.

What happened on a heart-crushing scale at Thu Thua happened in a thousand small ways every day all over Vietnam. We try to act out of principle, with good motives. But even the good that we do, and the good relations we build with people, become occasions for evil, like at Thu Thua.

Only when we align ourselves, our wills, and our actions with God can we maintain our integrity, resiliency, and sanity. When we know Him as the warrior God He is, we can say to the evil-doers around us what David said to Goliath,

"You come to me with a sword, with a spear, and with a javelin. But I come to you in the name of the Lord of hosts, the God of the armies of Israel, whom you have defied. This day the Lord will deliver you into my hand, and I will strike you and take your head from you. Then all this assembly shall know that the Lord does not save with sword and spear; for the battle is the Lord's, and He will give you into our hands." 1 Samuel 17:45-48

As Mop Det (fatso), I remember this encounter and will forever be somewhat Buồn (sad) because I know I will never forget the children of Thu Thua. I also know God's grace is sufficient to forgive me and I still marvel and wonder that God will forgive those of us who fought there. He is a good, good God.

Chapter 7

Final Firefight

Yea, though I walk through the valley of the shadow of death, I will fear no evil; For You are with me; Your rod and Your staff, they comfort me. Psalm 23:4

It was about 1800 hours, and the sun was already low in the sky. The "magic hour" of dusk can lull you into a false sense of security, and that evening, I felt very much at ease. I had taken out my beat-up old Stella guitar, which I often brought on the boat to help pass the time. We were too close to the riverbank, and the river was too narrow for me to have felt secure picking that old guitar. I was thinking of Brenda and quietly strumming some chords. I remember the incredible stillness and beauty of the evening as I sat there with my feet propped up on the twin machine guns. There wasn't a hint of a breeze.

Suddenly, a streaming *whoosh* passed inches over my head, and my heart stopped. I knew it was a rocket-propelled grenade known as an RPG-2. That was a shoulder-fired rocket launched from the nearby bank of the river. Also known as a B-40, it is an antitank rocket containing two separate explosive charges. The first charge is designed to pierce armor plating. But if you want to knock out a tank, you must do more than make a hole. So, a second projectile inside the first explodes after the shell has penetrated the target. The B-40 is often ineffective against a fiberglass boat because it can penetrate the fiberglass and then come out the other side of the hull without detonating.

The forward gunner was usually the primary target of the enemy's attack. If they could knock him out, they eliminated two very powerful guns. But the shooter missed me by about forty yards. I still don't know what happened to my Stella guitar. Perhaps in my panic, I tossed it overboard, out of my way. I never saw it again. I slid down from my perch on the guttering along the gunwale into the gun tub.

Small-arms fire began seconds after the initial rocket was fired, and ultimately, thirteen rockets were fired at us. You might wonder how we kept track of them during a firefight. Subconsciously, we'd learned to keep count to get an idea of the attacker's size, determine how dispersed the attack was, and figure out how many guys were firing rockets. These rockets were probably coming from two guys. They were fired too quickly to come from one gun. They were certainly too close for comfort, but once we got moving, we had a chance.

We moved away from the bank, turned back, and started making our firing runs. I shudder thinking of how we turned that boat around and came back into the attack. It would have been much easier to keep going, but our job was to keep returning. The other boat was going through it, too. They took seven rounds, making a total of twenty B-40s fired at us.

I was hit by shrapnel in my face on the lower left eyelid. It was a tiny piece of metal that embedded itself and hurt like fire. But I didn't feel anything wet, so I wasn't bleeding. That meant I was okay, although I was scared half to death. We made multiple gun runs until the enemy finally stopped shooting at us.

Every time I blinked, it felt like something was slicing my eye. I couldn't get it out, and it was bothering me. I needed some medical attention to remove it. So, we called in a medevac dust-off helicopter to lift me out. The captain would take the boat back to the compound to pick up more ammunition, and I would rejoin the team back at Tan An.

A UH-1D "Huey" helicopter carried me to the Mobile Army Surgical Hospital (MASH) unit at the army post on the other side of Tan An. The doctor found a tiny piece of metal in the membrane below the eyeball and carefully removed it. He wanted to put a patch over it, but I didn't like the feeling of trying to see out of only one eye, so I talked them out of the patch. They did give me something to stop any infection.

When I left, I asked if someone could provide transportation for me back to my compound so I wouldn't have to walk through town in the dark. I was anxious to rejoin the team because my adrenalin released during the attack had left me with the shakes. I was also nervous from the scare with my one eye. But they told me to walk. One guy, I remember, said, "Our motto around here is: Dogs and sailors keep off the grass; dogs and sailors can walk."

I was angry when I heard that, and, by dumb luck, I found a jeep out front with the keys left in it. Quickly jumping in, I drove to our compound but parked about a hundred yards upriver so that the evidence of my momentary "moral failing" wouldn't be too obvious. I was walking down the gangplank to the barge when Lieutenant Rambo stepped out of the command communication center about thirty feet to my left. The time was about twenty-two hundred hours. I started to greet him but didn't. He looked up, saw me under the light of the gangplank, and stared at me for a second as if he was shocked. Then he said, "Roever, what are you doing here?"

He must have thought that my patrol had never gone out, that we'd been in town screwing around. He was aware it had been known to happen. The punishment for playing hooky from patrol was severe, so I felt compelled to defend myself. I said, "Lieutenant, I've just come in on a dust-off. Sir, I got some shrapnel in my eye, and they fixed it at the army medical unit.

The guy was stunned. He said, "Roever, I know that; I just talked to you on the radio an hour ago, and you guys were under attack."

"Yes, Sir," I said. We had made one radio communication during the firefight, calling in a light-duty fire team, which means you get two or three helicopters for aerial support.

"I heard that firefight on the radio," said Rambo, "and when the dust-off was called in, I specifically heard that the side of your face was blown off, the trunk of your body had third-degree burns, and that your hands suffered blast damage. I heard that over the radio." He still looked at me in disbelief, as if I were a ghost.

Of course, I was stunned, too. I said, "No sir, no sir, I'm fine. I just got some shrapnel in my eye. Nothing like that happened. Everybody is fine. None of the other team members got hurt."

He came over to the gangplank, we shook hands, and I went into the barracks to lie down for a while. I thought my boats would be back in about an hour. I lay back and began to think how Lieutenant Rambo got that information. I didn't know the lieutenant's prophetic words would be true within twenty-four hours!

Chapter 8

Tragedy 07-26-69

For You have delivered my soul from death, my eyes from tears, my feet from falling. I will walk before the Lord, In the land of the living. Psalm 116:8-9

L ater that night, the boats returned, and my teammates came over to see how I was doing. They thought I was hurt far worse than I was. Their concern was touching. But our patrol activity was not over. We rearmed and refueled the boats, although we took our time doing so. You get very slow when you're back at the base, feeling safe and secure after having multiple B-40 rockets pass over your head and boat.

We took our time to have a big breakfast. We were not afraid to go back, but we didn't want to go back in the dark. We had to return to the point of contact because that's where the enemy would be. So, we delayed our departure until we knew it would be daylight when we arrived at the location. It was about 0400 hours when we finally left the base.

It's not easy to return to the exact place of a firefight because the jungle brush along a river can look the same for miles. We had to hunt for the spot, and in the chaos of a firefight, it's difficult to remember geography because you're focused on trying to stay alive.

We searched until we were confident that we had found the attack spot. I was behind the wheel, and I beached the boat myself. My teammate was on the forward deck, directing me where to pull onto the riverbank. Then I crawled through the chief's cabin. I ducked down, hurried to the bow, and stood up between my guns. I saw a bunker about twenty or thirty feet in the brush in front of us. Immediately I spun the guns around, not wanting to leave us unprotected.

When expecting the enemy, everything seems to move. I thought I saw movement in that bunker, but I wasn't sure because the brush was heavy. However, I realized the .50-caliber guns were elevated too high to hit the bunker. We weren't receiving enemy fire, but I was cautious, knowing the enemy had been firing rockets at us out of that bunker twelve hours before.

Although I could see the bunker, I wasn't sure which opening I was looking at or if it was, in fact, an open bunker. We were too close to risk throwing a fragmentation grenade; if I missed the hole, I could kill us all. I decided a white phosphorous grenade was the right one for the job. It would do two things. First, it would burn down the brush and expose booby traps or wires that might be strung around there. Since I wasn't about to get myself killed walking to a bunker to check it out, that was a compelling reason to use it. Secondly, it provided smoke that would give me some cover when I went to look in the bunker.

A white phosphorous grenade doesn't look at all like a fragmentation grenade. It is a canister about the size of a soda can, and the spoon's detonating mechanism hangs down the side. The M-67 fragmentation grenades in Vietnam were unlike the World War II kind that looked like a pineapple. They were round and smooth, with the spoon on the side held in place with a wire called a "jungle clip." After removing the wire, the spoon was held down by your hand when you pulled the pin.

When you threw the grenade, the spoon would fly off. It wasn't activated as long as the spoon was in your hand. You can even reinsert the pin. Inside the fragmentation grenade, a small trigger charge and a larger charge of composition "B" explosive are encircled by a tightly wound and compressed serrated stainless-steel coil. The outer casing breaks apart when the grenade explodes, and the coil shatters at each serration. Those little stainless-steel bits can easily penetrate a skull.

I remember carrying a dead ARVN soldier off the riverbank one day. I searched his body for what killed him but couldn't find a single mark. We stripped him to find the fatal wound. When I turned him over, his head rolled back, his mouth fell open, and I saw what had killed him. The roof of his mouth had a tiny mark, about half an inch long. His mouth had been open when a grenade exploded nearby, and a sliver of steel sliced through the roof of his mouth into his brain, killing him instantly.

A white phosphorous grenade called a "Willie Pete" is designed to burn away brush, clear the terrain, and kill the enemy with intense fire, not shrapnel. The casing will blow apart, but it is not designed to disintegrate into small lethal pieces. The explosive charge is the same as in the fragmentation grenades, but the purpose of the explosion is to ignite and spread the phosphorus, which splatters like molten liquid. This chemical burns white-hot at 5,000 degrees Fahrenheit and ignites when exposed to air. You can throw a phosphorous grenade in a river, and it will still burn. It spreads out and glows, and the water bubbles and boils. We carried those grenades not only to burn away surface vegetation but also to destroy our boats should we be captured or wounded so severely that we couldn't defend them. One grenade will reduce everything in a radius of about sixty feet to ashes.

So, I jumped out of the gun tub, grabbed a "Willie Pete" grenade from the ammunition box, pulled the pin, and lobbed it toward the bunker. It landed pretty close, exploded, and started to burn, but it wasn't as effective at clearing away the brush as I had hoped. I thought a second one would finish the job. Reaching for a second grenade, I noticed a small piece of phosphorus, about the size of a quarter, had blown back and landed in the gun tub. It was burning the fiberglass floor, so I got into the gun tub and kicked it around with my boot until it burned itself out. Everybody was alert and on edge because we didn't know if the enemy was nearby.

I stood in the gun tub, exposed above my armpits, and pulled the pin on the second grenade. I drew my right arm back about six inches from my face when suddenly and unexpectedly, I heard a massive explosion. It didn't sound like a firecracker, bullet, or gunshot. It was as if someone had reached up and slapped my ear very hard. First, I heard the slap, and then I felt the compressed air pressure on my ear drum for a split second. The explosion's concussion was so loud that it instantly deafened me. I immediately felt intense heat, but only on the parts of my body not directly covered with phosphorus. I felt no excruciating pain. I stood there for a second as the ringing grew louder in my right ear. Then suddenly, there was only silence.

I was wearing jungle fatigues and my black beret. It was made of thick felt and protected the top of my head from the initial blast and intense burning before it was blown off my head. Above the beret's leather brim line, I suffered only second-degree burns. Below that, my facial skin peeled off like a mask and landed in front of me on the boat's deck. Stunned and in shock, I looked down and saw one-half of my face on the deck. From my right eye, I saw only flames; then everything went blank. Out of my left eye, I watched, horrified, as the skin from my face shriveled on the deck like newspaper set aflame. I saw the ashes of my face swirl around in a circle and then float off into the air. The explosion instantly stripped the skin off the side of my head, neck, right shoulder, right half of my chest, and upraised arm.

At first, I thought we had been hit by a rocket. But it quickly dawned on me that my "Willie Pete" grenade had exploded. I remained conscious throughout the episode; indeed, I remember it with the vividness unique to traumatic moments. Time seemed to slow down, and my brain, which usually filtered out insignificant sensory information, retained every sensation and feeling. I saw my skin float away on the water's murky surface, and I felt myself beginning to go deaf and blind. I knew my clothes were on fire, and my hand was nearly severed. My right thumb was hanging down against my wrist. My skin was dripping off; and was pale white, covered with globs of burning phosphorus. The moisture in the skin was desiccated, sucked out, and my skin was peeling off. Underneath, I saw raw flesh. I recall the smell of my broiling flesh and the acrid garlic-like smell of phosphorus. I had previously smelled burning flesh, even rotting flesh, but this had a nauseating sweet odor. I retained my sense of smell, even though the right side of my nose was blown off, and all that remained was my left nostril.

I don't remember hearing anybody say anything. I knew I had to get out of the gun tub, and there was only one way. If I had tried to crawl underneath the chief's cabin, I would have blown everybody sky high. The ammunition box was there, and I, a living torch, would have ignited the whole thing. The metal container at my feet where I had gotten the white phosphorous grenade was dangerously hot. Incredibly, none exploded. Still, phosphorus covered everything. The deck of the boat was on fire.

I knew I had to grab the top of the .50-caliber guns and hoist myself up, even though I saw the guns were glowing red and white-hot from the explosion's blast. Still feeling no pain, I grabbed the top of the guns and tried to pull up. I was cooking my palms but didn't feel the heat. My hands slipped the first time, but I grabbed them again, mostly with my left hand but using my right palm and index finger. Somehow, I pushed myself up, leaned over the left gun, then rolled down onto the deck and into the water. It was the only thing I knew to do.

When I landed, I felt water rushing into my left ear. I could also hear the bubbling of my burning skin. Out of my left eye, I saw pieces of burning flesh floating off my chest. I didn't float to the surface. Instead, I drifted under the boat and was pinned between the keel and the river bed. When I felt the crushing pressure of the boat on top of me, I was certain I would drown. The thought flashed across my mind; *"Brenda will be permanently alone!"* I was being pushed face down into the mud, but the pressure was against my shoulders and the rest of my body, not against my head. I remember straining and pushing, trying to free myself. It seemed like a Sumo wrestler was sitting on me.

Then suddenly, the boat came off me, and I was free. I kicked my legs, propelling myself up from under the boat. When I surfaced, I faced the boat on the opposite side from where I had rolled into the water.After coming out of the water, my first words were, "God, I still believe in You!" Those were the exact words I yelled. I looked into the heavens and screamed, "God, I still believe in You," and thrust my left fist straight up. It must have been a wondrous sight to behold. I often question why those were my first words. However, that statement represents my mother's powerful influence in my life. Her attitude toward suffering was like Job's statement, *"Though God slays me, yet I will trust in him."* She never blamed God for her afflictions. Somehow, I recognized that my attitude at that moment – the moment of impending death – was crucial.

I was concerned that God might misunderstand me if I didn't say that. *"I want You to know I don't blame You for this."* I didn't want Him to be upset. I didn't want to let Him down. It was both a personal acknowledgment and a respectful statement. When meeting my Maker, I wanted to be familiar enough to call Him Abba, Papa, yet I felt tremendous fear and awe that required a respectful formality. I had come to Vietnam, not asking, "Why me?" I had come asking, "Why not me?" I wanted God to know my attitude hadn't changed; I was still submissive to His will. Of course, I knew that He knew my attitude – I wasn't going to tell God anything that He didn't know – but it seemed as though I needed to affirm it for my benefit. I was not fighting doubt. I was just maintaining the communion with a heavenly Father I had begun at sixteen. My mother's influence shows that the words I screamed paraphrased my mother's faithful cry.

There was a second significance to my cry, "God, I still believe in You." It was a statement also addressed to my buddies in defense of God. That may sound presumptuous – defending the ways of God to men in such a moment – but I didn't want to let them say, "Look what Roever's God did to him."

We had a new guy on board who had been in Vietnam for only a few days. When he saw me swim to the surface, still burning, bubbling, and glowing, he leaped into the water and quickly swam to me. I remember the strange look on his face: It was as though he had suddenly discovered war is hell; he had been dropped into an inferno, and his horrified expression seemed to say, *"This is going to happen to us all."* I turned in the water and started swimming to the shore. My finger was flopping uselessly, and large patches of my skin had become detached and were floating away with the current.

Bless his heart, the rookie followed me, swimming after me through fragments of my burning flesh. He kept tentatively reaching for me and stopped short of doing so; because he would have caught on fire. When I got to the river bank, I kept pushing against the mud, but I didn't know if I would have the strength to stand up or fall back into the water and die. I wanted to get out of the water. I was sure I would drown if I didn't. I was willing to die on the bank of the river but not in the water. I had realized by then that I would continue to burn in or out of the water. I wasn't afraid to die, but I didn't want to drown.

A more precise quotation from the Scriptures had come to mind. Paul's statement in Philippians, "To die is gain." In my mind, I began repeatedly saying, "To die is gain, to die is gain." I thought I would die, but death didn't present any threat — life did. When I reached the river bank, I realized God had told me I wouldn't die. He reminded me of the first half of that verse: *"For to me to live is Christ."* Over and over, I was saying, "To die is gain," yet, like an echo, I began hearing, *"To live is Christ."* To die is gain. To live is Christ. Suddenly I understood that my submission to God's will was a faithless wish to die. Subconsciously I wanted to die. I was much more afraid of what life would be like after the explosion than I was of death. I saw my face and skin turn to ashes and drift away in the light breeze and swift river current. My identity was trailing after them. When I said, "God, I still believe in You," I was thinking, *"To live is Christ"; I believe in You, so let me die."*

All these thoughts and feelings happened within mere seconds, but my conversation with God took place in the deepest part of my spirit. And in those moments, I came to know something of how Paul felt when he said, *"I am in a strait betwixt two, having a desire to depart, and to be with Christ; which is far better: nevertheless, to abide in the flesh is more needful for you."* Through the dialogue over the two halves of that verse, it was as though God were saying, *"I understand your desire to be with me, to escape the torment of recovery. But you must understand my desire. My use for you is not over."*

I realized that living in Christ from then on would be a kind of living death. *"To live is Christ, but to live in Christ is to die to the self and be crucified with Him – to be baptized by fire and water into His death before rising up from that baptism into His resurrection."*

In many respects, my life has been a living death since I cried out in the water. As soon as I get insensitive to that fact – as soon as I begin to think that *"to live is Roever,"* as soon as I start to get self-satisfied and begin to think that my ministry owes its success to my charisma, to my power and beauty – God reminds me that *"to live is Christ."* He reminds me that such a life is a crucifixion, a continual bearing of Christ's cross, a wearing of Christ's flesh just as He wore ours, a life of sharing the mocking, ridicule, and scornful laughter borne by Christ on the cross. We are to be "Crucified with Christ."

I'm still learning the lesson I discovered on that muddy riverbank in Vietnam: that the Christian life is dying to self; it's an ongoing crucifixion of one's own will. Deep in my spirit, I sensed, as I watched my flesh bubble and burn on that riverbank, that my disfigurement would forever keep me hanging on a cross. Rolling into the water and coming up on the other side of the boat, I had undergone a baptism of water, fire, and blood into the death of Christ.

I went under that water with one identity and came up with another. Stripped of my skin and face, I emerged clothed in Christ in a new way. I experienced in the flesh what every believer must learn: one must be stripped and clothed in Christ, but before one can be clothed in Christ's glory, one must wear the clothes of His shame. In this, each Christian experiences, in a small way, the action of Christ's incarnation, for He was stripped of His heavenly glory and clothed in corruptible human flesh so that our flesh might become incorruptible.

Splashing, burning, and profusely bleeding, I pulled myself out of the mud and leaned back on my thighs. There, crouched on the bank, I had a strange vision that may seem funny and irrelevant, particularly in the context of the previous theological statements. It was not a vision of Jesus or anything spiritual but one of my guitars. My folks had bought me a brand-new Gibson twelve-string electric guitar as a going-away gift. When I was in Vietnam, one of my daydreams was about going home to play that guitar. In my vision, I saw it on a stand in front of me. Crouched there, I said, "Guitar, I will play you again." I had just looked at my wounded hands, yet I said, "Guitar, I will play you again." The Spirit of God gave me hope. Amid the greatest defeat of my life, this apparition of good things appeared. Then suddenly, I fell backward, and everybody thought I had died.

The phosphorus continued to burn into my chest cavity as I lay on my back. It had mostly dripped off with my skin, but some had seeped into my body. A hole burned right through the little cavity above the sternum into the trachea, and I began to breathe through my chest. At the same time, I felt as if I were suffocating. My cheek was almost completely blown off, my jawbone was charred black and exposed, and my teeth were visible. My tongue had become so swollen that it filled my mouth cavity. I tried to speak, but nothing would come out. I had not yet felt pain because I was in shock. I had no sense of time. The guys gathered around me in a circle, one of them was packing mud on me to stop the burning, and Pervert Number Two was kneeling over me, praying. A teammate was lying beside me. His face, arms, and hands had second-degree burns. The phosphorus had set his clothes on fire, and jumping in the water had saved his life. I never did learn how the two of us ended up so close together on that riverbank.

I must have gone in and out of consciousness because the next thing I remember is hearing the whopping sound of helicopter blades and thinking how fast the dust-off had gotten there. The mud had not put out the fire, and I was still burning when the helicopter landed. They rolled me onto the stretcher, face down, thinking I was dead. They carried the other injured teammate over because he was still alive and then returned for me. Meanwhile, I had caught the stretcher on fire, and when they picked it up, it ripped open, and I fell out on my head. Then they rolled me up in wet blankets to suppress the flames. My skin was so dry; it was burning like paper.

Chapter 9

Medevac

*I cried out to the L*ord *in my great trouble and he answered me. I called to you from the land of the dead, and L*ord, *you heard me!* Jonah 2:2

I was barely conscious and remember little of being lifted out. I know the medic on the helicopter thought I was dead. When I faintly called out "Medic," the poor guy went bonkers. He thought I had come back to life. I said "Medic" because I was afraid he might stick my dog tags into my gums. That was the usual procedure with the dead. If the dog tags hang around your neck, they might break off and get lost, and you're unidentifiable. So, when someone dies, they drive the dog tags up between their teeth and gums. I was nearly blown in half but still conscious enough not to want my gums split. The medic was badly shaken, and the pilot tried to get him to shut up and settle down. I remember feeling the pilot had briefly lost control of the aircraft. The back end swung around, the helicopter quickly lost altitude, and I felt weightless. I thought, *"Oh God, we're going to crash, and I'll be the only survivor."* Black humor, perhaps, yet, it shows how I had begun to believe that no matter what happened, I was going to live. I was not going to die.

I begged for water. They couldn't give me any but finally, let me have little pieces of ice.

The medic tried to get some morphine into me, and I vaguely recall that he had problems – he couldn't find a needle for the syringe and finally just stuck the syringe itself into a wound in my leg and pumped in the stuff. It didn't do any good. When the helicopter landed, and I was unloaded, the wind whipped by the blades was like a bellows blowing hot coals, and I burst into flames again. Then I started to feel the pain.

While I was in transit, the verse, "To live is Christ, to die is gain," began to mix with a phrase from a secular song, "Walk like a man, my son," until the rhythm of my mind was *To live is Christ, to die is gain; walk like a man, my son. To live is Christ, to die is gain; walk like a man, my son.* Those phrases ran through my mind for days. They spoke little of the spiritual battles to come, the mixture of spiritual lessons to be learned, and the many habits of the mind I had to unlearn.

The helicopter flew me to a MASH unit, the Third Field Hospital. We arrived there on the date of my injury, July 26, 1969. The emergency room's first job was to put out the fire. They scraped it out of me, cutting my burning flesh away. Some of it had blasted deep into me, and as they cut out burned and blackened flesh, they found more phosphorus which burst into flame when exposed to oxygen. Incredible as it may sound, pieces of phosphorus were still smoldering twelve days later when they opened me up in Texas. They cleaned out the hole that had been burned in my trachea, inserted a plastic tube, and I breathed through that hole for almost a year. They gave me massive amounts of morphine, but that didn't stop the incredible pain I was feeling.

I heard part of a conversation not meant for my ears. One doctor said, "He's not going to make it." The guy on my right said, "I think we ought to try." The first guy thought they should spend their energy on the wounded who had a chance. The guy on the right said, "Let's go ahead and get the fire out." I felt like God, and the Devil were bargaining for my soul. Thankfully, the guy on the right won.

I stayed in the Third Field Hospital for two and a half days. They cleaned me up as best they could and managed to put out the fire. Then they loaded me on a helicopter and took me to Tan Son Nhut airfield in Saigon. Driving there, the ambulance stalled in heavy afternoon traffic. I recall lying in oppressive, suffocating heat, with nobody tending me until the drivers eventually started the engine.

I stayed at the Tan Son Nhut Hospital for one night, en route to Japan, where sophisticated burn treatment could begin. I don't remember anything of the night in Saigon. I also don't remember feeling any pain thanks to the drugs.

The next morning, hooked to an IV and still asking for water, I began the flight to Japan. My gurney was rolled out to a big C-141 medical transport plane, where I joined a long line of wounded soldiers waiting to be stacked inside. We were departing Vietnam, and although we were leaving the war behind, we still had many battles to fight ahead of us. Some would win, others would not, but all of us would be changed.

Chapter 10

Yokohama, Japan

Fear not, for I am with you; Be not dismayed, for I am your God. I will strengthen you, yes, I will help you, I will uphold you with My righteous right hand. Isaiah 41:10

I arrived at the 106th General Hospital in Yokohama, Japan, on July 29, 1969. A woman from the Red Cross came by to help me write a letter to my family. She wasn't very tactful in suggesting something like a final goodbye. Although, I admit there wasn't much cause for hope of me living.

I had suffered approximately forty percent third-degree burns from my waist up. That is massive damage that would require extensive recovery efforts. I was fortunate to have thrown the grenade while I was in the gun tub since it protected me from the waist down. Except for a few places on my leg where my pants had caught fire, my legs and lower trunk were not burned. If I had been standing up holding the grenade, the phosphorus would have coated the entire right side of my body, and I probably would have died within a few minutes.

At the time of my injury, I weighed 190 pounds. I weighed 130 pounds when I arrived in Japan. I'd lost sixty pounds of flesh and body fluids. The deepest burns were on the right side of my face, under my chin, and on my neck, not only from the blast and the phosphorus but also from my burning clothes.

I was suspended on a vertical bed that slowly revolved through a full circle, like the giant wheel where an expert knife thrower's assistant is attached. While she spins around, He throws his knives, outlining her limbs with the blades. In my case, the revolutions occurred once an hour; this process was repeated because a burn victim is subject to fluids filling their lungs, slowly reducing respiration until cardiac arrest occurs. Instead of knives being thrown around me, they were used to cut away my dying flesh in a process called debridement. My moment of darkest despair occurred in that hospital. A medic was foolish enough to hold up one of those magnifying mirrors in front of me.

"Oh my God, I am a monster, not a human being, certainly not Dave Roever," I thought when I looked at it. My face was covered with charred black skin and was swollen on the left side, almost to the width of my shoulders. I could see out of my left eye, but it bugged out of its socket.

The right side was nearly flat; a few scraps of dead flesh hung from the bones of my skull. Fluid oozed from the remaining flesh. There were a few places of swelling where the flesh still had circulation, but for the most part, my cheek was gone. There was an opening through my lower gums down to my chin and back to the muscle. I could see inside my head. My gums were charred. My teeth were black. My tongue was still swollen, filling the mouth cavity. I had no right ear, no hair, and patches of exposed bone covered my head, especially above my ear and at my eyebrow. The right half of my nose was missing, and I had only one nostril. My right eye was gray and lacked an eyelid. It was just a big gray exposed eyeball sitting there.

I also got a glimpse of the gaping hole in my chest. I saw the bumps on my esophagus and the tendons in my throat. I saw my ribs and organs moving around inside of me. Everything looked wet. The three outside fingers on my right hand were almost severed. Only one finger on my right hand was still attached. Somehow, my index finger was undamaged without even a burn.

I was struck with a lightning bolt of soul-searing pain when I looked into that mirror. I can tell you that being burned is a shriveling pain that makes you feel like you're being sucked into the air about you. My soul seemed to shrivel, collapse on itself, and be sucked into a black hole of despair. I was left with an indescribable and terrifying emptiness. I was alone in the way the souls in hell must feel. Jesus used the psalmist's words when He cried, "My God, my God, why hast thou forsaken me?"

After the medic walked away, I reached over, wrapped my little finger around the tube inserted in me, and yanked it out. I assumed it was my lifeline, filling me perhaps with the blood keeping me alive. I lay there, waiting to die, wanting to die, but nothing happened, except I began to feel hungry. I had pulled out the feeding tube!

I've never experienced despair as I did in those moments. Fear of rejection overwhelmed me. I found myself looking utterly repulsive. I could not and would not identify myself with the monster in the mirror. How could anybody?

My thoughts and fears were concentrated on Brenda. I was terrified that my wife would be ashamed of me. I couldn't imagine she could love me. How could I expect her to play beauty to the beast I had become? I thought, *"I will be a freak if I live through this. She is a young woman, barely twenty years old; too young to be stuck with somebody like me."* The thought sounded noble but was largely selfish because the worst possibility would have been seeing my young wife walking away with another man, arm in arm. Somebody who could care for her better than I would come along, and she'd take him.

What could anybody do with a life like mine? My lifetime of dreaming about being an evangelist burned to ashes and drifted away in that swiftly moving current of the Mekong tributary. Perhaps I could sign up with one of the touring freaks' shows. In my mind, I heard the barker say, *"See the fat lady, see the hermaphrodite, see the Siamese twins preserved in formaldehyde, see Roever."*

I was loaded with drugs and experienced an almost hallucinatory state of agony. I must consider these contributing factors when analyzing my guilt for attempting suicide. I was ultimately responsible, but I had lost my good judgment through circumstances beyond my control. I will have to wait until eternity to have it judged as God alone can judge. In the immediate sphere of the temporal, far from punishing me, He was rushing special graces my way.

When my family received official word of my injury, Mom phoned Paul Klahr, a missionary stationed in Japan, and said, "I have a son over there who's been severely injured. He's not expected to live. Would you please find him and just comfort him and pray with him?" He was on his way immediately. He found me on my third day in Japan and walked through the door twenty minutes after I had attempted suicide.

When I was at my lowest, I saw him walk up to me like an angel sent from heaven. I looked at this guy I had never seen before in my life and said, "You are a Christian, aren't you?" He said, "Yes, I am. I've come to pray for you." I smiled and said, "Hallelujah!" He started praying for me, and I fell sound asleep. My healing began while I slept. When I woke up, I was ready to live.

Chapter 11

BAMC San Antonio

I would have lost heart, unless I had believed that I would see the goodness of the Lord In the land of the living. Psalm 27:13

I was flown from Yokohama, Japan, to Randolph Air Force Base in San Antonio, Texas. Then I was transported in a caravan of ambulances to Brooke Army Medical Center (BAMC) at Fort Sam Houston in San Antonio, Texas. I spent four weeks in an intensive care unit and another eight months in the burn ward for skin transplant operations.

Thirteen of us, all burn victims, arrived together and were placed in intensive care Ward 14A. A couple of guys were already in there. I remember seeing one sitting in an old wooden wheelchair with all his skin burned off. He looked like living hamburger meat. They tried to feed him scrambled eggs, but he couldn't keep anything down. He died soon after we arrived. I had been wrapped in bandages for the trip – yards and yards of bandages. The nurse's first job was unwrapping me, which took an hour. When they pulled off the bandages, globs of stuff came off attached to them.

My fourteen months of hospitalization can be divided into three phases, although they overlap somewhat. For the first month or so, my survival was at stake. I didn't know what lay ahead; I didn't know how to think about the future, and I was in agonizing pain. A psychological turning point came on September 3, when I was taken off what was called the critical list: my official status changed from "very seriously ill" to "seriously ill." Thus began my recovery's long six-month middle phase, including fourteen major skin graft operations. These had begun a few days after I arrived at Brooke hospital on August 4. I was removed from the seriously ill list on October 10 and had two thirty-day convalescent leaves from mid-October to mid-November and from Christmas to the end of January 1970.

The last phase, when my recovery was assured and I could begin looking forward to life outside the hospital, started on March 10. I was finally taken out of the intensive care ward for specialized burn treatment and transferred to the regular burn ward. During April, I had a third thirty-day convalescent leave. A month later, I was transferred to the VA hospital in Dallas, closer to home, for a final four months of recovery, primarily as a self-sufficient patient, until my official U.S. Navy discharge in September 1970.

The long, tedious, painful period of fourteen operations required that I summon the resilience that had allowed me to withstand the physical ordeals of training on Mare Island and the psychological stress of the POW training on Whidbey Island. Indeed, I was now a prisoner as I had never been before, and my jailer was relentless pain and suffering. The pain usually places you in solitary confinement, which is one lonely place. Recalling the specifics of this hellish period, I am truly grateful that Brenda and my mother were by my side. Those two women knew how to sing in the dark; they filled my prison of pain with singing as Paul and Silas had filled theirs. Brenda and my mother were there, and I was not alone. In fact, Brenda's touch, as it communicated her love for me, seemed to take away part of my suffering. Something in "bearing one another's burdens" was not merely metaphorical but quite literal. In a real sense, she was afflicted with my infirmities to the depths of her soul. Her love enveloped that pain and brought happiness into a time of excruciating pain. I started to learn how to sing in the dark myself.

My most precious memory is of the first time I got to go home with Brenda to share the first night alone together since the night before my deployment. Brenda guaranteed my healing when she said, "Welcome home, Davey," but that guarantee was sealed, and my healing was largely consummated when she passionately took me into her arms at home. She had gone to great lengths to make everything perfect for this night. She wore the evening gowns and lingerie she had prepared to wear on our R&R vacation in Hawaii, which would have been a week after my injury.

I never thought I could put my ugliness out of my mind. It certainly seemed impossible to me that Brenda would ever be able to see beyond the horrible scars. Our first night together removed the fears and doubts about any of that. Alone for the first time, together on our marriage bed in our apartment, there was great spiritual and emotional healing that reached beyond my scars and touched my soul.

I wanted that woman so much! It was as though I could say to Brenda, *I love you, and I am still the man you married, and I am still the husband who took you home that first night when we were both virgins.* That night was as passionate and innocent as our first night of love because we had remained chaste during our separation. I felt confirmed by Holy Spirit in my resistance to the temptations of the flesh which the devil had set before me in Vietnam. I felt this renewed intimacy was God's blessing on our faithfulness. That night Brenda and I consummated our love as though we had never had the privilege in our marriage before. That was the beginning of the next stage in my healing process. In the hospital, Brenda's love had to be confined to her presence, words, brief kisses, and the touch of her hand. Still, when she could present herself, body, and soul and yield to me – embracing me and accepting my embrace -- only Jesus knows the full extent of how that night has shaped my destiny.

The beauty of Christ's love for the church is that He loves it even in its ugliness. Saint Paul tells the husband to love his wife as Christ loves the church, so I'm reversing the roles of the analogy here, but Brenda loved me the way Christ loves the church, even in its ugliness, embracing it as though it were the most beautiful bride in the world. His embrace makes the church holy, and Brenda's embrace made me feel worthy, a man with his dignity intact.

When I looked into that mirror in Japan, I felt sub-human, like an animal. I could not see the image of God in my reflection. In my training on Whidbey Island, when the specially trained officers' corps impersonated the North Vietnamese, the enemy tried to make you into an animal, to make you nothing but a creature with animal appetites, to arouse a man's appetite so much that he would forget his values. In a sense, my buddies in Vietnam played the same game. They also wanted me to become an animal to make sex merely another animal appetite. Satan took every opportunity in Japan to get me to consider myself an animal. He was often successful. When I looked in the mirror, what I saw could not be distinguished as human. I looked more like a dead dog run over on the highway. I felt a revulsion that demanded I deny who I was in the eyes of my Maker and Redeemer.

Brenda never ceased seeing me as a man who was made in the image of God. Physical appearances never blinded her spiritual eyes. Brenda loved me through her redemptive love, which convinced me that God's image was there no matter how I appeared to the world. As the administrator of grace, Brenda played the Christlike role in bringing me back to a full understanding of my dignity. Yes, our roles were reversed in Saint Paul's terms: Brenda became Christ, and I became His bride. But that's not so strange. As the embodiment of the church, whether male or female, we Christians all play the feminine role to Christ. We are the ugly bride made beautiful in His embrace. Likewise, in the priesthood of all believers, everyone plays the role of Christ, a member of His body, when they are the channel of God's mercy and grace.

My year of slow crucifixion required much of me, and I know it was as deeply painful to Brenda in another way as she watched me suffer and lived daily with my ups and downs. I could only have endured that year of suffering through the grace granted to me by God and the support of Brenda and my mother. I had no choice about the journey since I had few options. They were the ones who showed true bravery as they stayed close by my side through that tough journey.

It was indeed excruciatingly difficult, but it was not the hardest part. The hospital was an insulated, protected environment where I was surrounded by other people who were now "freaks." Being a freak was a common bond we shared, so none of us were singled out or ridiculed. Stepping back into the everyday world with everyday people brought new challenges and fresh harsh pain.

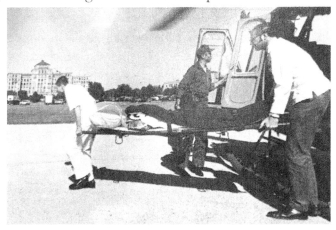

The Ministry – A Call to the Kingdom

"Becoming Dave Roever, the man of God I was created to be while living in the scarred body war had given birth to, was one of the most difficult challenges of my life."

"For God's gifts and His call can never be withdrawn."

Romans 11: 29

Chapter 12

Fort Worth – 2022

My people will dwell in a peaceful habitation, In secure dwellings, and in quiet resting places. Isaiah 32:18

The soft whine from Benny finally roused me from the deep sleep which had stretched for too many hours. "Okay, boy, I'm coming," I said as I rose from the bed and slipped my feet into my soft house shoes. I thought back to the last few days. As a resiliency coach for the Department of Defense, I was often scheduled for intense days in front of troops, and their faces always left an impression on my mind. The days had left their mark on my tired body, which resulted in a long night of sleep, but now the faces flashed into my thoughts. *"Lord, please take the seeds of hope I planted in their minds and let them take root in their hearts and lives."* The quickly proffered prayer gave me peace about the troop's welfare as I went into the kitchen and fed my hungry Cavalier King Charles Spaniel.

With Benny settled and a steaming cup of coffee on the table next to my easy chair, I pulled my Bible and morning devotional into my lap. Taking a deep drink from the mug, I prayed, *"Come, Holy Spirit, come. What does Abba, Father, want to say to me today?"*

I patiently sat in the comfort of His presence for a moment, simply relishing the awareness that He was with me. Finally, pulling on the ribbon that marked my reading place, I found the comforting reassurance from my Savior meant for me today. He spoke to me in the fourteenth chapter of John.

"Let not your heart be troubled; you believe in God, believe also in Me. In My Father's house are many mansions; if it were not so, I would have told you. I go to prepare a place for you. And if I go and prepare a place for you, I will come again and receive you to Myself; that where I am, there you may also be."

My first response to reading those words was to become aware of the sharp pain of longing to have Brenda still with me. Our mornings together had stored up memories of our moments of shared spiritual encounters with God as we prayed, studied the Word, and talked so deeply with each other about what He had revealed about Himself to each of us.

Then came the vision of her with Him in Heaven. The longing shifted from wanting her here beside me to my wanting to be there beside her. My mind began to consider what it must be like for her. *"He has given her a mansion."* I slowly shook my head from side to side, thinking about her life here. Remembering all the places she lived confirmed she certainly did not have any mansions here on earth; quite the opposite was true.

She had been born into a family with few material possessions and, by worldly standards, lived in poverty for many years. Oh, what a different place she lived in now. Brenda had never complained about her life here on earth. She never expressed any regrets or frustrations about any of it. Just thinking about how her life touched my heart caused tears to flow freely. They flowed not from the well of grief over not having her with me anymore but from the utter amazement that she had been my wife for all the years through all the hard things she endured because of them.

For over fifty years, I have traveled worldwide speaking and coaching others about the importance of resiliency while living with a woman who was its epitome. Only God could have orchestrated that amazing scenario. Looking honestly at her life caused me to reflect on all the elements that had given her a deep-rooted resiliency woven into her very character and personality.

Brenda's dad was a Choctaw Indian whose ancestors suffered tremendous loss as America was being settled. In modern times, their culture developed with stoicism at the core of their lives. The incredible pain coming down through the generations had caused rebellious anger and rage in the early generations, giving way to the stoic acceptance of all they could not change. Low expectations of outward greatness had developed an inner way of finding peace in the simple things of life. Out of necessity, the Choctaw's ability to be great warriors and hunters had slowly been replaced by calm lifestyles that found few outlets for their competitive natures. Her grandparents never had much beyond the treasure of a happy family life. A close-knit family, they were often gathered around the kitchen table where a cutthroat domino game of forty-two was being played. While her mother was not a Choctaw, she had adopted many stoic attributes that were the foundation of her married life. So, Brenda was naturally very reserved.

She did not have to be outgoing to attract me. On the first Sunday of my sixteenth year, I walked into my father's church in Lake Worth, Texas, and was captivated when I saw her for the first time. She sang in the choir, but I only noticed her beauty. Her hair, face, skin, and everything about her attracted me. The only put-off was the letterman football jacket she wore that day. I recognized the number of the star player emblazoned on the jacket. I knew he was only too glad to have this beautiful girl emblazoned as his also. There would be stiff competition to win her heart, but I was up to the task. As she started to walk away from the church that day, I addressed the issue head-on. I engaged her in some small talk, then, nodding toward the jacket, asked, "Are you dating him?" She fixed me with a look that set me down a notch and replied, "Duh," as she shook her head and walked away.

This was not the beginning I had hoped for, but I wasn't giving up. I heard things were not that solid with her and the football player. So, in a plan to minimize that first impression, I got my brother Al to ask Brenda out for a date. I asked out a sweet friend named Sherry so we could double date. The date night progressed, and as planned, Al and I switched places about halfway through the evening. I fell into step beside Brenda and began a fun conversation. Later, Brenda and I sat in the back seat as we went home. While the car was stopped at a red light, a guy in a pickup next to us threw a cigarette out of his window. It landed on the top of Brenda's bouffant hairdo. In those days, girls used a lot of hair spray to keep their "do" in place. Immediately, her hair caught fire, and I was given the perfect opportunity to rescue my "damsel in distress" by quickly putting out the flames. This was no swooning maiden, however. She thanked me for quickly helping her but was silent through it all.

A key element of resiliency is knowing who you are and staying true to yourself no matter what happens. It was always a key element in Brenda's life. At the night's end, I knew I wanted this woman in my life forever. I walked her up the steps of her house onto the wide front porch and stood under the light her parents had turned on. I mustered up all the courage I had in my sixteen-year-old self and did the only thing that made sense to me. I asked Brenda to marry me. Her beautiful face immediately registered a look of surprise, disgust, and then shock. It took a couple of seconds before she believed what her ears were sure they had heard. However, she did not doubt her answer once she quickly sorted it out. She slapped my face hard, conveying the proper amount of admonishment. Now that she was sure she had my attention, she said, "If you love me, you will wait for me."

Astonished, with a stinging left cheek, I thought, *"This is wonderful. She didn't say no."* If ever there was anything in my life worth waiting for, it was this beautiful young girl. Under the glare of the porch light so long ago, I had no idea how worth waiting for she truly was.

Brenda was thirteen, and I was sixteen when we met. For the next year and a half, we attended Lake Worth High School and got to know each other. This beautiful girl was very appealing to me, but her innermost nature was what attracted me most. Because she was so reserved, it was easy to tell that I was someone special to her when she smiled or opened up to me. From the moment she first did that, I was captivated.

Brenda was very popular in many ways. She was an academically high achiever and a very competitive basketball player. I remember several times when she was hoisted onto the player's shoulders and carried off the court because she had swooshed the basket as the buzzer rang out in the game's final seconds, giving her team the win. She had her pick of boys, but she chose me.

It is interesting to reflect that God orchestrated our being together. I had a cool Morris Minor convertible, a "chick-magnet car." I was into music, played the French Horn, had a Gibson guitar and was in the lab band. So, I, too, had opportunities to choose other girls. But my extracurricular activities were centered on Brenda. We didn't realize how important it would become in later years that we both knew each of us had chosen the other. We had looked around, and we both knew God had made us for each other.

In my last semester of high school, my family moved to the Fort Worth suburb of White Settlement, where my dad became the pastor of a church. That move rapidly increased the miles on my car's odometer, but she was worth every mile.

Her family accepted me and encouraged us to spend much time together in their home. Since I was a preacher's son, particularly their preacher's son, I probably had an advantage in the competition. They grew to know me while we dated for four years, and a deep relationship developed between Brenda and me. I spent a great deal of time at their house and became part of the family even before I officially was.

One day after dinner with her family, I dried the dishes as her mom washed them. It was such a comfortable place, and I enjoyed being there. Somehow, just out of the depth of what I felt in my heart for her mom, I said, "Helen, I love you." She dropped the plate she was holding, then ran out of the room into the side room. I stood there, wondering what I had done wrong. Questions flooded my mind. Did she think I was hitting on her? Did she misunderstand what I meant?

When she came back into the kitchen, she was drying her tears. Looking at her with genuine concern, I asked, "What did I do wrong?" Her reply was one of the most shocking statements I had heard up to that point in my life. She could not meet my gaze as she said, "We don't say those words in this house. No one has ever said those words to me."

There was no sense to be made out of that statement. I could not imagine that this house, where I was growing in love with Brenda and her with me, was not a house where people often spoke of their love for each other. I decided that I was going to keep saying those words. I said, "Well, Helen, I love you, Brenda, your other kids, and your whole family."

I was only sixteen when I asked Brenda to marry me, but our love and devotion were so real and evident that it changed how her family expressed their love for each other. They began saying they loved each other. The four years of dating were a time of devotion and commitment that grew with our shared experiences. In the beginning, Brenda learned to say I love you as our relationship grew. But from that day until she died, Brenda rarely said I love you first. She always responded but was not outwardly expressive of what she felt inside. Some people might judge that as a character flaw. However, God knew that some of what would happen over our time together here on the earth would create feelings with the power to overwhelm her if she focused on them. Resiliency sometimes requires us to be able to manage our emotions, so they don't manage our lives. He had prepared her well to walk the journey ahead.

Chapter 13

Becoming One

Therefore, a man shall leave his father and mother and be joined to his wife, and they shall become one flesh. Genesis 2:24

We had a very romantic four years while we dated. Occasionally we would drive to "inspiration point" close to Brenda's house. It overlooked a beautiful lake where the moon and stars shimmered overhead, the soft calls of night birds filled the air, and we felt drawn to the natural attraction God had given us for each other. We hugged and kissed, but we never had intercourse before marriage. I was a typical boy madly in love with this beautiful and alluring young woman. There was no denying I had the urge to "merge," but she would quickly cool my jets.

She was strong in her faith in a God who asked for sexual purity. She was firm in her resolve to honor Him, herself, and our relationship. She was pure in her heart and stayed pure physically. I am so grateful for her strong morals and character because our marriage was founded on God's deep, abiding things, not something that happened in the back seat of a car. She knew the Scripture from Hebrews 13:4, "*Marriage is honorable among all, and the bed undefiled; but fornicators and adulterers God will judge.*" She would say that she wanted to serve God and please Him, and she didn't want to bring down His judgment on us.

At long last, on July 15, 1967, Milton David Roever, at the ripe age of twenty, and Brenda Louise Draper, age eighteen, made a holy commitment before God, standing in my dad's church, Lakeway Assembly of God, and we became husband and wife. It was a beautiful ceremony and celebration, filling us with incredible joy and anticipation of all that was to come.

Thanks to my brother-in-law, Travis Williams, the very next thing that came was a little stinky. As my bride and I drove away from the ceremony and went toward the hill county of Texas, we became increasingly aware of a very unpleasant odor. We found out sometime later that Travis and some of the guys put Limburger cheese under the car seat and smeared it on the engine. The more I drove, the worse the smell became. We laughed at the antics and knew it was a "rite of passage" young couples often must endure.

When we got to Kerrville, Texas, we went to The Hill Country Inn. The simple inn was a beautiful place we always remembered with deep fondness. Because we did not have pre-marital sexual relations, our honeymoon was beautiful and very special. It was a time of newness and wonder as we came together as one. As often as I can, I encourage young people to stay pure until their wedding. It is a once-in-a-lifetime experience. Unless they have waited, they will never know the incredible joy of an undefiled marriage bed, which a wedding night can genuinely be. We also went to Natural Bridge Caverns, which was just being developed, then drove through the hill country, enjoying the scenic views. Mostly we turned the page in our life book and started our new chapter as husband and wife.

I knew from the beginning that Brenda was precious and what a blessing God had provided me by giving her as my wife. I wish I could have given her a mansion to live in and all the desires of her heart. But that wasn't going to be our life. When we returned to Fort Worth, we lived in an apartment above an electric company owned by a friend.

I worked at General Dynamics and rode my motorcycle to work each morning. Brenda bravely took on the role of a married woman. She wasn't the greatest cook when we started our married life. When she made my breakfast, I couldn't tell the difference between the potatoes and the gravy. But the eggs were dressed up for breakfast and had lace on them. We had a lot of laughter and fun over her attempts at cooking before she got the hang of it.

Preferring not to enter the military as a draftee, in 1968, I enlisted in the Navy. I was sent for basic training at the Nimitz Naval Training

Center in San Diego, CA. There was a Mission ship placed in the parking lot where we trained. I always joked that I would have jumped off and broken my legs if they said to abandon ship. However, I completed it without incident and was ordered to report to the Great Lakes Naval Station in Waukegan, Illinois.

Brenda's attitude was that wherever I was going, she would go too. I installed a hitch on the back of my Mustang and pulled a tiny U-Haul with all our earthly belongings behind the car. When we first got there, we lived in an apartment. It was tiny and nothing fancy; indeed, not a mansion. The best thing about it was that the lady who owned the house had a poodle we loved. The dog would go crazy trying to bite a bowling ball she had. We would laugh until we cried watching him.

Once, we did get to live in a mansion on earth. It wasn't ours, and it was only for a short period. In Kenosha, Wisconsin, we were in a big house on Silver Lake that belonged to the Assemblies of God church we were attending while I was stationed there. We had an arrangement with the church that we could live there for free if I restored the house. The lake was the most beautiful I had ever seen. No matter its depth, it was so clear that you could see the bottom of the lake. We spent beautiful moments together walking or sitting on the pier, which went sixty feet out into the lake. The house had sixteen rooms and a fireplace so big you could stand up inside it.

My job was to restore that beautiful old mansion the best I could. There was much to be done. One of my big projects was to strip all the floors and revarnish them. We loved our life there in that earthly mansion, but I'm sure it falls far short of what is planned for us in Heaven. Reflecting on Brenda now having a mansion brings a smile to my face. I'm sure hers doesn't require all the work we did in Kenosha!

My grade point average was the highest in our class when I finished training. The admiral congratulated me and handed me my diploma. Papers clipped to it were my new orders. I was to train at Naval Amphibious Base in Coronado, California, to become a Brown Water Black Beret and immediately deploy to Vietnam. The path from that earthly mansion led the way to the hardest goodbye I would ever say. One that would forever change our lives and require a depth of faith and resiliency that no young couple ever expects to face. Brenda was not allowed to go to California since I would live in the barracks and be involved in training. She returned to Fort Worth and lived with her parents.

The Navy trained us hard and prepared us for what was to come. As it got closer to the time of our deployment to Vietnam, we were told that our team had the highest killed in action (KIA) per capita in the war. They explained that it couldn't be proved because most of the guys killed in our group went down with the boat. In that situation, they were listed as missing in action (MIA) since their bodies could not be recovered to prove they had died.

I never told those dark facts to Brenda because I didn't want her to know I wasn't coming back. Standing in Love Field on the day of my deployment, in my heart, I thought I was kissing her for the last time. I promised her I would come back without a scar to reassure her. It was a promise I felt I would surely break. When the plane landed in Vietnam, I saw the caskets being brought back to the USA and thought to myself, that is the way I will come back home; in an aluminum container. Later, she told me about the day she thought that I would indeed come back in one of those containers. I recalled the look in her eyes as she talked about it, and in my mind, I heard her quivering voice, which was profoundly sad.

Chapter 14

U.S. Navy Notification

Be anxious for nothing, but in everything by prayer and supplication, with thanksgiving, let your requests be made known to God; and the peace of God, which surpasses all understanding, will guard your hearts and minds through Christ Jesus. Philippians 4:6-7

Brenda recalled, "Dave, that sunny Texas Sunday on July 26, 1969, was one of my loneliest days. Going to worship alone always seemed lonely. Our love of God and worship of Him was such a deep connection that I somehow felt incomplete sitting on the pew without you. That morning, I sensed the warmth of having your arm around my shoulders and smiled when I remembered how you would gently touch my hair. I struggled to focus on the worship and the message because the ache caused by your absence was so powerful.

Thankfully, as the service ended, I focused on returning home with Mom and Dad and the normality of Sunday dinner. After the meal, we settled into our usual quiet Sunday afternoon. Soon I would realize that it was the last normal or peaceful time I would know for a very, long time.

Watching a blue military car pull into the driveway, I had an overwhelming feeling of dread in the center of my being. Wearing white Navy uniforms, two men bearing the worst news I would ever hear walked to my door. Leaving no room for me to refuse it, they pressed a yellow telegram into my hand. It was more than I could bear to listen to the man's words, so I clutched the awful message and rushed to my room, trying to process what was happening. Through flowing tears, and while holding my breath, I read:

"Mrs. Brenda Louise Roever; with concern, I confirm on behalf of the United States Navy that your husband, Milton David Roever, GMG3, B72 83 61, USN is very seriously ill, with third-degree burns to the face, neck, arms, hands, and right cornea; and tracheotomy. His prognosis is guarded. These injuries were sustained on the Van Co Tay River; in the Republic of Vietnam when a white phosphorous hand grenade accidentally discharged during a routine river patrol. Your husband is presently hospitalized at Third Field Hospital, Saigon, C/O Air Post Office, San Francisco, California 96307, where you are assured that he is receiving the best possible care and treatment. When further reports are available concerning his condition, you will be promptly informed. The anxiety this report brings you is fully understood, and I join you in the wish for his recovery."

I rushed straight into the arms of our All-Mighty God. I poured out my loneliness, fear, and pain from knowing what you were going through and my heartbreak that you were so far away and alone. On the floor that day, I invited Him to feel, hear, and know what this had done to me. After a while spent with him, I found that I could breathe again, and slowly I felt His peace. My prayer brought two requests; *"Lord, Dave is my best friend, and I don't want to go through life without him, so please let him live. And, Lord, I want to be like you, so please let me see my husband the way you see him; let me not see the scars; please always let me see the man you made and gave me to cherish. Amen"*

I received a telephone call every morning for the following seven days. Each one assured me your condition was grave and death was imminent. On the eighth day, I received word they were sending you to San Antonio, Texas. I was told to wait until they said I could see you, but I was in the waiting room of your ward in Brooke Army Medical Center when your medical helicopter landed at Fort Sam Houston.

It had been eight months since that momentous day at Love Field in Dallas when you held my tear-stained face in your big strong hands and peered into my soul with those blue eyes. Remember, you whispered that you would be back without a scar. Now I stood at the entrance of hell, the door of the intensive care unit. The nurse positioned herself in the center of the entryway. I could see you. But you could not see me. The wounds were extremely severe, and the man I saw was barely recognizable as a human being.

Forced by love, my heart drew me close to your side. From your waist up, you were covered in a creamy white medicine. Your head was swollen to the width of your shoulders, and gaping holes left by missing and torn flesh riddled your chest and arms. Black, burned flesh showed through from under the white salve. The strong hands gently caressing my face a few months earlier were misshapen and mangled. The face of the man I married two years earlier disappeared behind a curtain of charred flesh. I knew the recovery period would be slow and painful, but that became secondary. You were home; my prayer had been answered. Davey, I was so glad you were alive! I did not marry you because you were handsome or had a great body. I loved you because of your character, kindness, gentleness, goodness, faithfulness, and capacity to love. None of those traits were damaged, destroyed, or scarred by that grenade."

Hearing her tell me of her journey pierced my heart because no one wants their wife to go through what she went through. It also reassured my heart of how deep her love for me was. A love like the love Brenda had for me worked miracles for my recovery.

Chapter 15

View From Death Row

But we have this treasure in earthen vessels, that the excellence of the power may be of God and not of us. We are hard-pressed on every side, yet not crushed.
2 Corinthians 4:7-8

I am deeply grateful that I didn't come back in one of the aluminum caskets; however, the way I returned required much greater strength and resiliency for a longer time for my beautiful bride. I had no choice about walking down that path. I still marvel that this sweet, innocent young woman choose to remain on that path with me. She chose to stay but refused to let this great tragedy diminish or destroy her or our relationship. That is the true sign of resiliency. Sadly, not many people possess it the way my wife did.

When I was in Brooke Army Medical Center's burn unit, I saw that not all wives chose to stay. I was placed in an ICU ward that patients knew as "death row" because all the people there were beyond any possibility of survival. The amount and severity of their burns made it highly unlikely that they would live. Out of the thirteen of us, I was the only one who survived.

The guy in the bed beside mine had third-degree burns over one hundred percent of his body. He had no hope of survival. No one with burns that severe had ever lived. At best, he had only days to live. His remaining days would be filled with unbearable pain and extreme discomfort. His wife came in one morning, took off her wedding ring, and threw it on the bed. She stood there and said with total disgust, "You are an embarrassment. I couldn't even walk down the street with you." This woman was overcome by the horrific change that had come into their life. She lacked any resiliency to rise above the situation to hold on to the greater good. The woman's actions scared me more than any enemy action ever had.

Now, I was faced with the possibility, or probability, that my beautiful young wife would react the same way. I knew she loved the man I was before I left for Vietnam. I was petrified that she could not find that man here in the charred ruins of my body.

Brenda, her parents, and mine were there waiting, but only Brenda came in for the first visit. I had felt wrapped in the arms of God since Paul Klahr's visit, and I longed to see Brenda. Still, I was also tremendously anxious, as if the tracheotomy hadn't been performed yet, and I was suffocating again. I waited for her to walk through the door, wondering how she would react when she saw me, what the expression on her face would be, and if she could accept me. I felt as though my whole future, identity, and life depended on the look on her face when she saw me.

The nurses tried preparing patients and loved ones for these unhappy reunions. Few of us were expected to live, and few of us did. We were all hideously disfigured. Monsters, really. The nurses didn't walk our loved ones straight to us. They took them the long way and showed them other patients first so that the husband or son in question would not present the shock he otherwise might. I imagined Brenda thinking, *"Thank God, that's not my husband,"* until the thought occurred to her; *"maybe my husband will look worse."* Nothing prepares people for the sight of burn victims.

When Brenda walked in, she was gorgeous and more beautiful than I had ever seen. She wore a hospital gown, but under it, I could see she had dressed up for her man. In an instant, I saw that she had remained faithful to me, lived for me, and kept herself chaste for me during those months of separation. The memory of her love had kept me away from all temptations; it had kept me from violating her trust, and, somehow, my first feeling upon seeing her was of her worthiness and fidelity. She was worthy of the virtue and the purity she had inspired in me. She was beautiful and possessed an inner radiance from her relationship with God.

The nurse brought Brenda to the ward and walked her to my bed. After several seconds she said, "This is not my husband." Those words reinforced my deepest fear. She couldn't see me for all the horrific carnage. The nurse gently explained that it was me, then showed her the identification bracelet on my arm. Standing a little taller then, Brenda looked deep into my one good eye and, with a big smile, said, "Well, it is you after all! Welcome home, Davey. I love you!"

Her unique name for me sent an electric shock throughout my body. It was as if every cell in my body had been waiting to know their fate. That simple phrase sent hope into my soul and life into my cells. I looked at Brenda and said, "Baby, I'm so sorry I can't look any better for you than this." I'll never forget her answer as she grinned and said, "Don't worry about it, Dave, you were never that good-looking anyway!"

Now, that's resilience. She loved the man she dated for four years, married, and became his other half. The scars, the problems, the pain, and the uncertain future didn't shake her and diminish anything about our lives together. That's resilience personified and on steroids.

I was in the hospital for a year and two months, and it was a great blessing to be able to then walk out with my suitcase in one hand and my sweetheart in the other.

Brenda never criticized, complained, or screamed about how unfair this was. The doctors told us I would never be able to father the children we had begun to dream about and plan for. She accepted the reality of what our life was now; however, she immediately began to fight for all the possibilities of what it might become. Our God is a God who fights for us and alongside us. Oh, by the way, on March 30, 1971, our son Matthew David was born, and then Kimberly Michele was born on June 12, 1973. We have two living-proof miracles to show that nothing is impossible with God.

Chapter 16

The Hut

The righteous cry out, and the L̲ord̲ hears, and delivers them out of all their troubles. The L̲ord̲ is near to those who have a broken heart, and saves such as have a contrite spirit. Psalm 34:17-18

Quonset huts were built next to the hospital for temporary family housing and are a permanent fixture at Fort Sam Houston in San Antonio, Texas. Since World War II, they have been used for military housing and administrative offices. They were also frequently seen in movies depicting that era. The building's floor plan was simple.

A hallway ran down the center of the rounded structure with small private rooms on either side. A single bathroom at the end of the hall serviced all the occupants.

Brenda's Quonset hut entrance had a solid core interior wooden door with a screen door outside, which had a spring that loudly squeaked and "twanged" when opened. Temporarily occupying the hut were families whose loved ones were in the hospital's burn unit. These families lived in suspense daily, hour by hour, fearing their loved ones would take a turn for the worse and die. Frequently, patients died in the middle of the night, and their death was signaled by the loud clatter of the screen door opening with its twanging spring. Then with startling wakefulness, the families listened to the footsteps of the duty officer, chaplain, and attending physician as they walked down the hall, praying the approaching entourage would not stop at their door.

Although people credit me for my strength to survive the grenade explosion, I never feel comfortable or at peace with that. The families are the ones who paid a heavier price than I did—none more dearly than my young wife, Brenda. The gut-wrenching fear caused by the hut's squeaking screen door opening would quickly send the barely 20-year-old off her bed and onto her knees. Facing the door in her small quarters in the ancient Quonset hut, hands clasped tightly together in prayer; she quietly whispered, "Angel of Death, don't you dare stop at this door – not this one!"

Years later, she told me the following story. "The long, lonely night was beginning, and my heart was pounding in my chest as I lay on the tiny hard bed. I was sweating profusely even though the air conditioner purred a steady sound. My tossing and turning had pulled the thinning sheets from the corners of the military-style bed. My mind was flooded with the day's events, and my racing imagination was hard to control. The "what-ifs" ruled my thoughts.

The stark room where I spent countless lonely hours was plain with dirty white walls; its only furnishings were a dresser and a bed. There were no pictures, no mirrors, nothing to convey the warm, comfortable feeling of home. The room was simply lodging for families needing a place to lay their tired bodies down and quiet their troubled minds.

The screen door squeaked as it opened and then slammed back against the doorframe. I heard the heels of the shoes as they walked on the wooden floor. I rushed to my door, praying desperately that the footsteps were those of a family returning to their quarters. Yet, I knew they were not. *"Please, dear God, don't let them stop here!"* My soul cried in anguish as tears ran down my face. I slumped to the cold floor. *"Not at my door tonight! Not at my door!"* The scene would be repeated countless times as the Angel of Death hovered just out of sight. Once, I believe I saw his shadow, but he never stopped at my door."

Brenda's unwavering relationship with God and the strength drawn from the words of the Bible found in Psalm 28:7, *"The Lord is my strength and my shield; my heart trusted in Him, and I am helped."* carried us both through the most challenging times of our lives. Our constant prayer was based on Psalm 31, *"I trust in you, O Lord, I say you are my God."*

God gave us hope when there seemed no reason to hope. He gave us strength when it seemed there was none left in us. He gave us *"beauty for ashes, the oil of joy for mourning, the garment of praise for the spirit of heaviness; that we might be called trees of righteousness, the planting of the Lord that he might be glorified."* Just like he promised he would in Isaiah 61:3.

His constant presence carried us through the long grueling days of healing and rehabilitation at Brooke Army Medical Center. The healing process for burn patients is a very unpleasant experience that takes immeasurable strength and resiliency for them and the loved ones on the journey with them.

Chapter 17

Keep It Together

But as it is written, "Eye has not seen, nor ear heard, nor have entered into the heart of man the things which God has prepared for those who love Him.
1 Corinthians 2:9

Brenda was not just occasionally there to visit me during those many months; she was with me during the entire process. Her attitude was amazing and did so much to help me heal. It was not the typical attitude found in that ward. She was stunned and saddened when the ward chaplain came to her in the first few days. He had divorce papers drawn up for her. He explained that it was the typical reaction of wives in this ward, and he just wanted to make it easy on them. Brenda was furious with him. It was inconceivable that a wife would leave her husband at the point of greatest need in his life. To the chaplain, it seemed impossible that a wife would stay. It seemed impossible to me that she had remained, particularly on the tough days. The love she showed me reminded me of what God had caused to grow between us, bringing immediate comfort and reassurance.

Skin is an insulator that keeps the body's heat stabilized. When burned off, the body consumes calories at a high rate trying to maintain proper body temperature. To stay healthy, I had to eat plenty of high-calorie foods. The problem was that I had no appetite. The trauma had shut down that natural desire for food. My doctors were patient but knew the time had come for some tough love. They brought in a large tray of food and insisted I eat it. They said, "If you want out of this hospital, you will have to eat your way out."

Brenda took up their mission with her usual manner of finding a way to get it done. She came in every day, and rather than telling me to eat; she fed me. At the time, I was on a massive number of painkillers. They were crucial to my recovery but often left me dazed and confused. However, nothing kept Brenda from ensuring I took in the food necessary to get enough calories. Sometimes she would tell me to chew when I wasn't aware enough to know she had placed food in my mouth. She never lost patience, got frustrated, or let the process become as tedious as it truly was. She also realized that the food being served was part of the problem. She began to bring me good stuff like hamburgers, candy bars, malts, and pizza. Always focused on solutions, not problems, she would cut hamburgers up into bite-sized pieces when I had skin grafts which rendered me unable to open my mouth wide enough to bite into them.

Amazingly, she also knew that the intimate contact that was always so special between the two of us would do a world of good toward helping me heal. She openly showed her affection for me and rekindled my desires for her. She once told my doctor that if he let her take me home with her one night, she would do more for me in that one night than he would be able to accomplish in a year.

That sweet young girl did things that would have been difficult for even the most hardened health care worker. She learned how to be a scab picker. As the skin was healing in its lower layers, the scabs and the dead skin needed to be peeled off from the top layer. She never shrank back from touching any of this. She gently and patiently did as she had been taught, never tiring or complaining.

On nights when I could not sleep because of the discomfort and pain, I would find Brenda next to me on the bed, gently dragging her fingers across my skin. Back and forth across my body, she would stroke and soothe. Her touch brought peace and comfort to me, and I would finally be able to drift off and get some sleep. She would give up her sleep so that I could get mine.

Truly the best gift in my life has been knowing Jesus Christ as my Lord and Savior. Having a woman who loves Him, too, as a faithful, dedicated wife has brought me more joy than I could have ever expected and certainly more than I would ask for.

At my lowest point, she rose above the horror of what she saw and found the man she loved. She looked past the insurmountable problems and found solutions. She stood with resolve and resiliency and refused to be defeated by any circumstance. I don't know what she was thinking through all of this; I can't imagine what she felt. Whatever happened, she met it head-on with the attitude she often expressed to us all, *"Keep it together; there are things to be done."* When we were struggling down the road back to health while at Brooke Army Medical Center, we had no idea that God was putting in place an amazing ministry to entrust to us during the next fifty-three years, Brenda's lifestyle attitude was vital in aligning with God and letting His will be done in the ministry. And oh, what wonderful things have been done!

Chapter 18

Beginning Ministry

Preach the word! Be ready in season and out of season. Convince, rebuke, exhort, with all longsuffering and teaching. 2 Timothy 4:2

My identity became an overwhelming issue the moment I stepped out of the hospital into the "real" world. Because of the skin grafts, the bad side of my face looked like the ball at the tip of a roll-on deodorant bottle. It was just an expanse of smooth, featureless skin giving me the appearance of "Mr. Marble Head."

Slowly walking down the hallway the first time I left the burn ward, I passed a woman with young twins at her side. When they saw me, they went wild with fear. I couldn't blame them. I was pretty hideous to behold. The left side of my face was bright pink because the top layers were burned off, but the basic skin was still there, looking as if it were sunburned. On my right side, the eye was covered, the ear was gone, cartilage stuck out from my nose, and my face was blood red from the new skin graft. Half my mouth was sewn together, so I also talked funny. The two young children looked and pointed at me, screaming, "Mommy, what is it? Mommy, what is it?"

There is no person in the word *it*. Their question caused me the sharpest pain I had felt since I had looked in the mirror in Japan. I looked at them and said, "It is a man, kids," and continued walking away.

I realized I had to accept a new identity that included my freakish appearance, and I'm still not completely comfortable with it. Every year, with each new operation, I have gained the ability to see myself with the outer disfigurement, yet I know that who I am is not limited by how I look.

Even while I was in the hospital, my desire to preach had come back to life. When I could hold a Bible again, my parents gave me a beautiful red *Thompson Chain Reference Bible*. My dad handed me the gift, saying, "This is a good study Bible for you and your ministry." It was his way of opening up the vision he knew was God's calling on my life. "You can begin to prepare messages from this great study tool."

"Why should I prepare a message if there's no place for me to preach?" I asked.

"Well, why would you be given a place to preach if you don't have a message?" In his gentle way, he had reached into my soul and peeled off a scab of self-pity. He treated me the way he saw me; a man with a vocation and a calling in his life. That attitude prompted me to revive the vision as well. Sitting at the bedside tray table, I wrote two sermons.

Shortly after, one of my faithful visitors, a pastor named James Brothers, walked into my room. After we visited a little, he gave me a precious gift that could have only come from God. He invited me to preach twice at his church in a few weeks. I immediately accepted, even though I knew I wasn't allowed to leave the hospital and would have to sneak out.

"When do you want me to pick you up?" he asked.

"Very early Sunday morning would be perfect."

I worked on my messages and gained confidence with each day. Early Sunday morning, wearing my hospital robe, I crawled past the nurses' station to avoid detection. I clutched my study Bible and the only clothes I had to my chest. My clothes were a pair of old blue jeans and a pajama top. The only shoes I had were the hospital-issued flimsy slippers. Having awakened before sunrise, I was undetected in the dark as I ducked behind a tree and pulled on my blue jeans. When pastor Brothers pulled up, what a sight greeted him. I was standing in jeans, a pajama top, a robe, and slippers, with one eye and one ear. My skin was fresh looking and so delicate that if you pushed on it, it would come right off.

I will never forget that morning at his church. We arrived early, and I sat on the front pew with my back to the congregation and my left arm resting on the back of the pew. Only my left profile was visible; it was red but not distorted.

Pastor Brothers invited me to the front to speak. As I rose and walked to the pulpit, people became aware that I was wearing a hospital robe, not a coat. When I reached the pulpit, turned around, laid my Bible on it, and faced them, they were shocked. Several women put their handkerchiefs to their mouths and ran for the ladies' room. I stood there thinking, "*God, why did I do this? Look at what I did to them.*" I heard satan's voice whispering in my ear, "*You monster. You know you are a monster. Look what you are doing to these people. You are a freak. It will always be this way. You've missed your calling, buddy. You belong in a circus sideshow*".

Even with the devil standing close by, the Word of God in my heart began to minister to me. *"Faithful is he that calleth you, who also will do it."* With those words came new strength. I put the whole thing into my Father's hands. I started to preach. That morning, I didn't tell the people about Vietnam. All I did was preach Christ crucified. When I finished preaching my message, I offered an invitation to the congregation. Big, burly men walked down that aisle, tears streaming unashamedly down their faces, giving their hearts to Christ. I knew then that my ministry had begun.

These R-COM (Roever Communications) trucks house state-of-the-art equipment used to produce "The Dave Roever Crusade," a weekly television program aired on the Trinity Broadcasting Network.

Chapter 19

Early Days

God has saved us and called us with a holy calling, not according to our works,
but according to His own purpose and grace which was given to us in Christ Jesus
before time began. 2 Timothy 1:9

I was discharged from the Dallas VA hospital in September of 1970. The day of my discharge was not as much a driving away from someplace as it was a time of going forward. What compelled me forward was the calling in my life to be a preacher of the gospel of Jesus.

The calling was strong, yet other forces in my life held me back. The struggle I had was being able to define what that life would now be. While in the Navy, the military set my schedule, duties, goals, and timeframe. Then I was in hospitals where my days were lived out in response to my physical health requirements. It was now time for me to take over once again and determine how to spend my days and, ultimately, my life.

Becoming Dave Roever, the man of God I was created to be while living in the scarred body war had given birth to, was one of the most difficult challenges of my life. Some days brought me to my knees as I fought through self-criticism and self-doubt. My belief in the Bible as the inerrant Word of God was the bedrock of my faith. There, I found a way to take my mind off all the "self" and live from my soul. Still, my strength was fragile at first and brought many opportunities for me to give up and walk away.

Unfortunately, one area where I needed a great deal of growth and improvement was how I responded to Brenda. The unconditional love she showed me in so many different ways was still unbelievable. When there is no self-love for the person you have become, it is hard to believe that someone else can love you. One look in the mirror reminded me of the disfigured person, who was now her husband. I couldn't look past the man in the mirror and see that I was created in the image of God; therefore, I couldn't believe that she could either.

I began to develop a destructive emotional pattern in our relationship. It was a passive-aggressive manipulation that I often used to get my way when her opinion was different from mine. If she didn't want to do something the way I wanted, I would say, "Well, I don't blame you; I couldn't love me either." She would never respond at all. I knew it was awful to say that to her, particularly considering all she had done to show that she loved me. I realized that behavior was terrible and knew I shouldn't do that to her. However, knowing what is wrong doesn't always lead us to do the right thing. I persisted in that response until it finally came to a head one day.

We were trying to scrape up the money to buy a house. She started talking about getting a job to earn extra income to contribute to our savings. I felt extremely threatened by the idea of her going out in the world daily. She would undoubtedly be around men who were far more attractive than me. One day, the discussion blew up and became a quarrel. I drew out my usual weapon to get my way and loudly said, "I don't blame you; I couldn't love me either." She didn't respond, and her silence spoke volumes to me.

That was it! I grabbed my coat, stormed out of the house, and jumped into the old truck we used as a second vehicle. My driving reflected my anger as I flew down the driveway and took off down the road. I had gone only about half a mile when I realized a car was approaching behind me and quickly closing the distance between us. As it got nearer, I realized it was her in our Ford Torino. The fact that she had followed me made me even madder. I pulled to the dusty side of the road, got out, and slammed the door. She pulled in behind me. When I walked to her car, she waited while the whirling dust settled, then slid the window down and peered up at me.

"Where do you think you are going?" I demanded.

"I don't know. I always go wherever you are going! Where are you going?" Her question was asked with a tone of frustration.

"I'm just getting away from you!" My terrible response was one of the worst things I have ever said to someone—especially the love of my life.

"What have I done to make you want to get away from me?" The question came from a heart genuinely trying to understand our problem.

"Brenda, every time I say, I don't blame you; I couldn't love me either, you don't answer me. I guess that means you don't love me. Now, you want a job so you can get away from me. That's why I'm getting away from you! But I don't blame you. No one could ever really love me."

She came out of that car, came up to me, and stood on her tip-toes until we were nose-to-nose and eye-to-eye. "You want me to say something? You want me to tell you why I never said anything? It's because the ignorance of that statement didn't deserve the honor of an intelligent reply."

Stunned by her honesty, I threw my arms around her and held on tight. The reality of the enormous effort she had put in to show me how much she loved me flooded my heart. Without using words, she definitely proclaimed her love for me to me and to the rest of the world. There could never be any doubt about her love because her actions broadcast it daily.

My relief, comfort, and exhilaration of knowing how much she loved me were powerful, but they soon became overshadowed by my guilt. How could I have treated her this way?

I stepped out of our embrace long enough to say, "Brenda, I swear to you before God and heaven this day, I will never again use those words against you." Then I entered her embrace, that place where she offered unconditional love to me. This time, I finally began to accept her gift.

Being able to accept unconditional, undeserved love was an essential step on the road to preparing to share the gospel. When I let go of the limitation I thought my scars had placed on my life, the possibilities of how God might use me to reach others flooded my soul. Brenda's unconditional love strengthened my belief in Jesus' love for me. The scars are only temporary signs of a worldly battle. I know Jesus sees the true me that was untouched during that firefight.

In a darkening world, many people have been scarred by the raging war of sin that is all around them. I began to pray that Jesus would let me see everyone who came into my life the way He sees them. I asked for the ability to show unconditional love just as I have felt it. My experience taught me that without that type of love, there is no hope. Knowing this has strengthened my resolve to carry the message into the world.

God's plan for each of us is put into place throughout our lives. Little things seem insignificant, yet they open doors to bigger things at the appropriate time. When I was sitting in my house trailer one cold January day in 1971, there was a knock on the door. Little did I know that when I answered the door, I would be opening it to one of those bigger things God had planned next in my life.

Standing on the doorstep was the man who had significantly influenced my teenage years. He led youth camps across South Texas every summer and included me in them. From when I was twelve until I turned eighteen, he treated me as an apprentice and introduced me to the prominent church leaders in Texas. Those times were invaluable to my professional development.

When I saw Laurell Akers standing on my doorstep that day, tears of sheer joy filled my eyes as I threw my arms around him. Having him in my house brightened up the gray day. We sat and talked for a long time that afternoon. I persuaded him to stay for dinner to enjoy the chicken-fried steak dinner Brenda prepared for us.

After dinner, his mood became serious. Sensing the shift, I asked, "Laurell, what brings you to Fort Worth?"

"Well, it's somewhat strange, Dave," he said. He looked away and struggled to gather his thoughts into the words he wanted to say next. He finally seemed to settle on how to approach whatever this subject was, so he blurted out, "I'm not walking out of that door. I'm not leaving here until you promise me you will be the associate minister at my church."

Stunned, all I could muster was, "What? What did you just say?" It wasn't that I didn't hear him. It was just that those words he spoke were being translated inside my heart and my head to say, *"Dave, I love you, and I have confidence in you. Nothing will change your dreams or keep them from coming to pass."* He repeated his bold statement using a more assertive tone than before. "I'm not getting off this couch, walking out that door, or leaving this house until you have promised me you will be my associate pastor."

"Well, Laurell, just move in because I will not be a pastor." I couldn't see myself being able to fill that role. He kept the conversation going until I finally asked, "What would I do?" He said, "I need somebody to help me understand my church's hurting people. I need somebody to minister to the people who suffer, somebody they can trust. You're the right man for that role."

Sitting very still, I thought, *"Dear God, he wants me. Somebody wants me."* My body was still, but my heart and soul were racing wildly with joy. A dark voice wanted me to say, *"No, no, no."* While every part of me was screaming my answer, *"Yes, yes, yes!"*

I didn't want to appear desperate or to convey that I thought he was my only hope to be able to minister. My pride held back my answer, letting him beg for a little bit. I said, "Let me pray about it."

Immediately, he said, "Let's pray right now." He wasn't a man of inaction. We prayed, and the Lord brought peace and joy to my soul. It sounded too good to be true.

Turning to Brenda, I asked, "Baby, what do you think about it?"

"Davey, it's a chance to get started." She knew if she used *"Davey,"* I would attempt anything. "Davey, just try it." Her encouragement pushed me over to their side.

"Okay, Laurell, the answer is yes."

"Hallelujah!" His high praise for Jesus caused me to know he had spent time in prayer before he came to ask me. "Let's make some plans," was his call to action. We planned until late into the night, and he left for his Houston home early the next morning.

Within a couple of weeks, we sold our mobile home and moved to Houston in our little travel trailer. We set it up in the parking lot, which became our permanent new home. The church greeted us with genuine gratitude, and I began preaching on Wednesday nights. I received no pay for being the assistant pastor at the tiny Glad Tidings Assembly of God church. However, he paid significant dividends for my healing soul by letting me preach. As I put on my coat and tie to preach the gospel passionately to this loving church, I gained a sense of dignity again. Until then, I thought it had been scraped off of me with the dying skin.

I supplemented our household income by taking a job as an office manager in the concrete coring company where my brother worked. There was a sharp learning curve since I had never had an office job, but I mastered the skills, and it supplied ample money. My real job was still preaching, which also began to pay off. Soon other pastors in the area started calling and inviting me to speak at their churches. They asked me to come and tell my story, usually for a Sunday night service. Before long, I was making good money from my day job and the extra money given to me on the weekends.

God showed His faithfulness which is written about in 2 Corinthians Chapter 9:8-9

"God is able to make all grace abound toward you; that ye, always having all sufficiency in all things, may abound to every good work. As it is written, He hath dispersed abroad; he hath given to the poor: his righteousness remaineth forever. Now he that ministereth seed to the Sower both minister bread for your food, and multiply your seed sown, and increase the fruits of your righteousness"

As I continued sharing my story with other churches, the requests for me increased. Sharing the hope God had given me when I had no hope seemed to call me forth to share it even more. The more He called me to share it, the more my hope of being able to fulfill my calling increased. His word is always faithful and true.

One day, Laurell looked at me and said, "You know you are not being a very good assistant pastor when you are gone all the time."

"And you know that you intended for this to happen." He smiled big as he met my eyes with a knowing look.

My time as associate pastor at Glad Tidings Assembly of God drew to a close, and God opened another door. Brenda and I began traveling as evangelists with Karen Crews. I first knew her when she was a teacher in my elementary school. Her heart had been drawn to ministering to deaf people, so she had formed a choir that sang in sign language. She had about fifty kids who signed in her choir called Signs for the Harvest Singers. They drew a big gathering, and Karen wanted an evangelist to bring the message. It was a perfect fit for me and the message God had given me. We always pulled our travel trailer everywhere to have a place to call home as we traveled around the country.

Despite the doctors' grim prediction that I would be sterile, we had recently had our first "miracle" baby. When Matthew was born, he was indeed a fulfillment of my heart's desire. He showed us that God's hand was on our lives, and He was blessing us. Matt also brought great delight and wonderment at having this tiny, perfect creation given to us by our loving Father. It was vital for me to have my family together while we traveled.

When we were near Laurell's, we would stop in for a visit with him. We would park at his house for a few days, and I sometimes preached for him on those occasions.

One morning, Laurell and I were sitting at his kitchen table, drinking coffee and talking as we did every day. The Vietnam War continued, but everyone saw that the end was near. The American troops were going to be withdrawn soon. Laurell suddenly stopped, put his cup down, looked across the table at me, and said, "You know, Dave, when Vietnam is over, your ministry will also be over."

It was the most astonishing statement anyone had ever made to me. He implied that my identity, my calling, depended on circumstances half a world away. I thought he was suggesting that I didn't have much to say except as a sympathy-raising, blood-and-guts testimony of wartime faith and courage. In my mind, I thought he was prophesying the eventual failure of my ministry. He seemed to say that he believed my identity as an evangelist was fraudulent.

God did not create me as a scarred, weak man who only represented fox-hole faith. How could my best friend, shepherd, and mentor see me that way? The pain I felt at this seeming betrayal was intense. I pushed my coffee cup away, shoved my chair back so suddenly it tipped back, coming to rest at a forty-five-degree angle against the wall behind me, and then forcefully, I rushed out of his house. I stomped into our trailer and yelled to Brenda, "Baby, we're leaving."

Unaware of the situation, she called back, "Oh, do we have another meeting?"

"We do have another meeting, in fact, lots more meetings. We won't ever be back here. I will never darken his door again!"

Stopping in her tracks, she sought my eyes as she asked, "What happened?"

"He just told me my ministry will be over when the Vietnam war is over."

Brenda didn't say anything. She sat where she was, quietly thinking. I backed the car around, hitched up the trailer, and we got back on the road.

We traveled for over a year with Karen Crews and the choir. The connections I made reinforced that I was doing what God had called me to do. After I spoke, pastors often brought me an invitation to come to their church for a meeting. Many times, I was invited to stay for several weeks. Soon, Brenda and I had a full year of booked engagements where I would bring a message of hope to people. Only God could have orchestrated having a full calendar of bookings only three years after I was released from the hospital.

He blessed us with our second miracle baby in 1973 when He gave us our beautiful daughter, Kimberly. The joy of having her in our lives filled my heart with gratitude. Shortly after she was born, we heard Bernard Johnson, an evangelist from Brazil, speak. He frequently spoke about the work the Lord was doing overseas. Whenever I heard the word overseas, my heart translated it to Vietnam.

Along with the profound gratitude after Kimberly was born, I believe the Lord also placed a new direction for my calling in my heart. We stopped at a red light when we left the meeting that night. As we sat waiting for it to change, I looked at Brenda and said, "Sweetheart, I believe God spoke to me tonight." This precious helpmate the Lord had given me looked into my eyes, saw my heart, and said, "You're going back to Vietnam, aren't you?" God had given her the same word, so she was not surprised.

The desire to go back as a missionary evangelist grew stronger each day. When I was there in 1969, He had placed a sadness that comes when we see people living without the love of the Lord in their hearts. Now, He was calling me to be part of changing that for everyone who lived there. Earlier, when I had been there, I carried an M-16. Now my great desire was to return carrying John 3:16. The first one tore their country apart; the second one would reconcile them to God.

Once we committed to returning to Vietnam, we saw an increase in the offerings and honorariums we received. I would mention the mission as I spoke in churches, knowing God would prompt hearts that wanted to support what we wanted to do. At a church in Crockett, Texas, a little old lady came up to me after the meeting. She explained that her husband had recently died and left her a considerable amount of money. She looked at me seriously and said, "I've wanted to support ministries when I am led to, and I would like to underwrite your trip to Vietnam."

I grew up believing in the importance of giving money to widows, not taking it from them. She was surprised by my response. "Thank you so much for the commitment and the love and support you are offering. However, I must say no to your very generous offer. I appreciate it, but God has shown me that He doesn't want one person to be the sole supporter of His mission over there. He wants to unite several people to work together. He will reward them richly when they follow His prompting. A modest investment would certainly be appreciated if you would still like to contribute." She protested my decision, but ultimately, I talked her out of her large donation.

The pastor had been standing nearby and heard this conversation. When he walked me to my car that evening, he said, "Roever, you're incredible. I've had four evangelists in this church who came here to talk her out of her money for their big-time ministries. Now, when she is ready to give it to somebody, he won't take it. That is about the most amazing thing I've ever seen."

The Lord had been testing me that night. He wanted to see if I would trust Him to sponsor that trip. When I was talking to the lady, I sensed Jesus standing there, shaking His head no. He was sending Holy Spirit to lead me. He wanted to know if I would follow Him to bring about His ministry or turn my way to build my kingdom. I chose to follow Him.

The entire trip's cost came to ten thousand dollars, including three months of living expenses for the time I would be there. It flowed in easily and quickly. I was able to leave in January of 1974. That was a difficult decision and a hard goodbye because I was leaving my family and would be away from them for a long time. I was compelled to make the trip because I knew the Lord had the same heart for the people of that country that I did.

I stopped in Japan on my way to Vietnam. I never forgot about the missionary who had spent three days of his family time tracking down a kid he didn't know. When Paul Klahr met me at the airport in Japan, he asked me what was behind my trip. "Well, sir, I came for only one reason. I wanted to be able to look you in the eyes, shake your hand and tell you how much it meant to me for you to find me at that terrible time of my life." Extending my hand, I said, "Thank you for coming to me, praying over me, and bringing me hope."

That expression of gratitude was sincere. I felt the way the one cured leper who returned to thank Jesus must have felt. Paul's emotional response was a huge blessing to me. It was clear he was deeply touched. It was a reminder of how important it is to let other people know how much we appreciate what they do for us. Paul was involved in some evangelistic meetings, so I stayed in Japan for a couple of weeks, helping him with those. It was a blessed time for us both.

When I arrived in Vietnam, I connected with several wonderful pastors working there to bring the gospel to the country. I began working with several men connected with Teen Challenge to help solve the Vietnamese drug addiction problem. The military finally admitted that it was a problem, not just for the civilians but also for the soldiers. The first efforts there to build a detox center were truly not designed to help the addicts. Over time, they built a better, more effective facility. I established some military contacts because of my service, which helped build better relationships as they worked to solve the drug problem.

I connected with local pastors who helped me preach in small churches in cities not controlled by the communists. During this trip,

I visited a new refugee village built by the Assemblies of God. They did far more than send in pastors. They were meeting the needs of the people caught in this great human tragedy unfolding in their country. Once their physical needs were met, the people were very receptive to hearing the driving force behind the work of the creators of their refugee village. I preached three services, each of which had about three thousand Vietnamese. The response was tremendous as God worked in their hearts.

Soon the money we had raised had been spent, and it was time for me to return home. This first trip solidified my heart's passionate desire to continue working in Vietnam. I sensed this would be the first of many trips, which made leaving them a little easier. I missed my family terribly, and I was happily waiting to be back with them. My family in Texas and I were much too close to each other to be this far apart.

Later, when I returned to Vietnam, I made Japan my base and brought Brenda and my children with me. Once settled there, I made trips into and out of Vietnam to continue my work. It had become evident that the communists were taking control of more cities. However, I would still find cities not yet fully controlled by the communists where I could preach a message of hope to the people.

On one of the trips, I went into Da Nang, where substantial communist control was evident. In one meeting in a bombed-out building, there were five hundred seventy-three Vietnamese Buddhist students. They were curious about my appearance. In their polite way, they asked, "What happened to you, sir?" It was the perfect opening for me to give my testimony. I told them I had come initially as a soldier to their country because I believed they had the right to be free, just as the Americans, the French, or the Japanese do. "But freedom never comes without a price," I said. I explained that I'd been severely injured when a grenade blew up in my face while I was fighting for their freedom.

The Vietnamese are very tender-hearted people. These young men had tears dripping from their chins, indicating the Lord was touching their hearts. Then I said, "I want to tell you about another man who fought for your freedom because He cares so much about you. His name is Jesus Christ. He does not let your good health depend on luck. He's not going to let your tomorrows depend on chance. God has a will for your life. This Jesus fought for your freedom. He was murdered in His thirties because His life threatened those who didn't believe Him when He said He was the Son of God. They killed Him. He died to liberate Vietnamese students just as much as He died for Dave Roever. He died to liberate the whole world from the captivity of our sins. However, He rose from the dead. He is alive, and He is here tonight. Jesus is in this place right now." These guys leaped to their feet and frantically looked around for Him.

"No, no," I said, "not where you can see Him with your eyes. He's here in Spirit. You can't see a spirit, but the Spirit of Jesus Christ is in this place." I continued to explain how Jesus could be with the Father and be with us, that we are the body of Christ, and whenever we gather in His name, His spirit is with us. Those young men were enthralled and could not have been more attentive.

At the end of the message, I said, "I'm going to invite you to accept Jesus. To show that you are ready to invite Jesus into your heart and life, I want you to stand to your feet, come forward to the front of this building, and let that be a symbolic statement that you are willing to leave your old Buddhist traditions, your godless religion of good luck. It will mean that you are willing to say, "Jesus Christ, I believe You are the Son of God, and I commit my life to You." When I gave the invitation, the entire audience en mass came forward, and I was dumbfounded!

I said, "Go back and sit down." They sat down. I said, "You don't understand. Make sure you understand. No rice is going to be given to you. No new home will be given to you. No money will be given to you. This is not a ticket to America. I am only saying that you will be forgiven of your sins and evil deeds, and you will be changed in a way that will make you want to forsake your old ways and accept the new ways of Jesus Christ. You will be given a Bible, and you should study it."

"Now, all of you who truly understand and still want to make this commitment, come forward."

Again, all five hundred seventy-three got up and came forward. I knew I had to make sure they all understood what they were saying by coming forward. Once more, I asked them to all sit down and listen carefully. I went through the salvation gospel again, carefully explaining each step. They began to giggle at me and then acknowledged they did understand each point I made. It was clear this time that they did understand. When I gave the invitation, they all came forward. When I led them in the sinners' prayer, and they confessed their sins, there were no dry eyes. Their tears were the outward expression of their inward sorrow about their sins and of the joy of their newfound salvation. That night, five hundred seventy-three people accepted the Lord Jesus as their personal Savior.

Saigon fell not long after that night. I was there on another trip for the same purpose as before when it fell. I scrambled to get out amid all the chaos and confusion. God's favor put me in the airport at just the right time to get aboard what was possibly the very last plane to get out of the city.

I had been back in Texas for about a month when I held a meeting in Lufkin, Texas. One night after the service, the pastor and I hung around talking. I needed to get to bed, yet something kept me there, just talking. When the phone rang in the church office, Rev. Freeze said, "Probably a wrong number. Nobody could be calling the church at this hour of the night." The phone kept ringing until he finally said, "Well, I'd better answer it. Maybe it's urgent." He fumbled for his keys, dropped them, and finally got the office unlocked. The phone was still ringing. He answered, and it turned out to be a person-to-person call for me from my friend Aaron Rothganger, the pastor who worked with Teen Challenge in Vietnam.

Aaron said, "Dave, I've just returned home, and I'm calling from Springfield, Missouri. I thought you would want to know: Seventy of those 573 people who accepted Christ that night in Da Nang have been executed because of their faith. They're your babies." That's the way he put it. "They're your babies."

I slammed the phone down. I was so mad at God I almost wanted to curse Him. I stormed out right past Rev. Freeze and said, "I'll see you tomorrow." He didn't have any idea what was going on.

Our little travel trailer was parked beside the church. It was late, and Brenda and the kids were already in bed. I slammed the door.

At that point, I didn't care who I woke up. Walking over to the full-length mirror, I grabbed my shirt and ripped it right off. Buttons came flying off, ricocheting everywhere, even off the ceiling. I frantically got the shirt off my body, exposing all my grotesque scars. Standing there staring at them in the mirror, I yelled, "Now, God, tell me it was worth it. If something good had come out of it, then maybe. But this is just Thu Thua all over again. How could you let this happen?"

I was so mad that I went over and fell on the bed, bouncing Brenda halfway off the other side. I put my face in the pillow and screamed at God, "You're not fair. You're not fair. You're not fair." My chest vibrated from these half-growling screams that came right from my soul.

God began to soothe me. It had to be His Spirit that touched my heart. *"Where do you think those seventy are?"* The Lord asked me.

I lay there exhausted and said, *"Well, I guess they're in heaven."*

He asked, *"Where do you think they wanted to be?"*

I remembered the little hooches where they had lived as refugees in squalid poverty. They lived with disease and malnutrition. They lived with the sound of rockets, machine guns, and mortar fires, in the devastation of the fire, and with the scars of fire. I said, *"God, they are where they have always wanted to go. I'm the one still stuck here."*

The verse that kept me alive in my moment of death came back to me as I prayed for these new martyrs of the faith, *"To live is Christ, and to die is gain."*

The Scriptures in Revelation 6 reassure us of what happens to the martyrs:

"⁹ When the Lamb broke the fifth seal, I saw under the altar the souls of all who had been martyred for the word of God and for being faithful in their testimony. ¹⁰ They shouted to the Lord and said, "O Sovereign Lord, holy and true, how long before you judge the people who belong to this world and avenge our blood for what they have done to us?" ¹¹ Then a white robe was given to each of them. And they were told to rest a little longer until the full number of their brothers and sisters, their fellow servants of Jesus who were to be martyred, had joined them."

These words show the love God has for them all. We can know we will see them again when we get to heaven. In the meantime, they are loved, cared for, and honored while living with God in Heaven.

In the five years since I stormed out of Laurell Akers' kitchen to start my ministry, I had been all over the country, all over the southwestern United States. I had been to Vietnam as an evangelist and had preached in Japan and Thailand. Our ministry had become self-sufficient and financially sound. The Vietnam War was over, and my ministry grew by leaps and bounds.

I returned to Vietnam to bring a healing message and minister to the wounds of war and drug addiction. While there, I realized that American GIs, veterans, and American students needed the same message as Buddhists and ARVN vets. I was one of the thousands who had gone over there. I was one of the thousands who had returned wounded, scarred in body and soul.

One early morning when I was in college, as I listened to the news of the war on the radio, I felt responsible for those fighting the communists in Vietnam. Now, I realize my responsibility was to those Vietnam vets fighting suicide, despair, lost ideals, drug addiction, joblessness, resentment, and rejection at the hands of wives, friends, and country.

I was scarred in my body but beginning to feel whole in spirit. Why? Because I had come home to hear "Welcome home, Davey; I love you." from the lips of a wife who had remained faithful. I received the same message from my family, church, and Lord. I had begun to realize that what Brenda had given me, I, in turn, needed to give to my comrades who had returned without hearing, "Welcome home."

The withdrawal of the American troops brought a new dimension to our ministry. I knew I was to bring a message of resiliency, strength, and encouragement to the returning veterans as they brought their broken and scarred bodies and broken and torn hearts back to their homeland. We increased in areas of ministry, helping with their transitions back home, their marriages which had forever changed because of military deployments, and their often-overwhelming response to traumatic events that impacted their hearts, minds, and souls.

As all of this was beginning to take shape and grow, I took pride in having proved Laurell Akers wrong. One day we were driving through Houston, pulling our Airstream camper behind us, when I looked over and saw a phone booth. It had to have been the Lord who put these words in my mind, *"Stop and call Laurell Akers."* When I believe God says something to me, I try not to argue. I swerved onto the exit ramp off Interstate 45 and stopped in front of the phone booth. "What are you doing?" Brenda asked.

I said, "I'm going to call Laurell."

"You're kidding."

I put in the dime and dialed his number. When he answered, I said just one word, "Laurell."

Without hesitation, he replied, "Dave, I thought you'd never call." It was as though he had been sitting by that phone for five years. He asked, "Where are you?" Once I told him I was in Houston, he said, "Come over immediately."

I hung up and got back in the car. As I started the engine, Brenda asked where we were going. I said, "To Laurell's." She didn't say a word in reply.

I pulled up the long lane in front of his little church. He was living in a house trailer next door. As I walked up, I noticed the door was open, as if I had just walked out of it. When he heard me at the door, he said, "Come in."

The kitchen table was only a few feet away from the front door. I immediately noticed one chair tipped back against the wall at a forty-five-degree angle. On the table was a half cup of coffee sitting in front of the tipped chair. Laurell was sitting across the table, watching me.

Not wanting to spoil what I knew he had done on purpose, I sat down and started sipping my coffee without saying a word. After a moment, he said, "Well, what do you think? Will the war's end finish you?

"You made me mad," I said. "Five years ago, you threatened me, and you questioned the one scrap of identity I had. While you were at it, you jeopardized the deepest friendship I've ever known. You put a challenge in front of me. I walked out of this place, opened my Bible, and built my ministry on the Bible to prove that I could build my ministry on the Word of God, not on a mere testimony about Vietnam. And I did. I beat you, Laurell." He quietly met my gaze and replied, "You beat me, Dave."

His demeanor and the look in his eyes brought new awareness to my soul. Five years earlier, he had said what he did to make me respond the way I had. He knew he was in the position to push this fledgling out of the nest so I could fly. Laurell had won. The Lord Jesus had been glorified. "Laurell," I said, "Laurell. . ." No more words came. I had none to describe the deep feelings I had.

"Boy, it took you long enough to figure that out. I've missed you, Buddy."

When he said that, I threw my arms around him and sobbed. Laurell loved me enough to risk what I now understood to be the deepest friendship in his life.

Chapter 20

Middle East Ministry

[He] comforts us in all our affliction so that we will be able to comfort those who are in any affliction with the comfort with which we ourselves are comforted by God. – 2 Corinthians 1:4

Being a Purple Heart awarded combat-injured Vietnam Veteran has been a major factor in the Department of Defense requesting that I travel worldwide speaking to military units about resilience, survivability, and inner strength. The following story is about my traveling to Iraq after Saddam Hussein was captured when U.S. forces took part in the Global War on Terror.

***

(The following story is an excerpt from the book "Scarred" last published in 2015.)

They call it "Battle Rattle." It is heavy, and it saves your life. The helmet is Kevlar, and the vest is bulletproof. . .maybe. The war is real, and the danger is ever-present. Going into Baghdad, Iraq, the C-130 did a combat landing, circling down in a spiraling motion to avoid rockets and gunfire from the crowded city below. The noise inside the aircraft was deafening, but my mind was trying to stay focused.

We landed, and the odyssey began. His bomber jacket and pistols on both legs lent his image to that of General Patton of World War II vintage. His head was shaved; his jaw was square, and his eyes penetrated to the soul. He was there to welcome me to Iraq. The colonel was quick to flash a smile with just enough tilt in his head to make me realize the welcome could come in a plethora of ways, and indeed, it did. My feet were hardly on terra firma when the first appointment was an eye-opening, mind-bending, heart-rending reality check.

First stop was the mortuary. The sad eyes of the young soldiers working at the mortuary told an unprintable story. The slight growth of beard and hint of red eyes told of weariness and heartache. Still, they tried to put the best faces on their soul-sapping job of tending to the war dead, which day after day sucked the marrow from the bones of their soul. I closed my eyes but could not stop my tears. I did not know that the hurt of war was only just beginning to be revealed to me that day.

Then, we were off to the hospital. We raced through Baghdad at a very high speed in a convoy armed to the teeth with armored Humvees before and aft. Our arrival was timed with the arrival of five casualties from an IED (improvised explosive device) or a roadside bomb, if you prefer. Two were dead; two had bullets through the neck, and the fifth soldier had incurred 100 percent burns over his body. I was rushed into the makeshift operating room, where the desperate attempt to save his life was a frantic exercise in futility. "Mr. Roever, pray for him? Please!" the doctor asked, never looking up from the intense effort to stabilize him. "I met you years ago back home at Dover Air Force Base when you visited us during your tour with Billy Graham," he continued. "This one is bad. I don't think there is any hope for him, but we will try our best."

I prayed. I wept. I knew that I would be doing a lot of both for the next week to come. I was right. My heart beat in double time. Memories raced through my mind. I had not seen such terror in injuries since my own from the phosphorus grenade explosion in Vietnam. My prayer was simply put. . . "Oh God, this medical facility no longer remains a hospital, for today, it is a hallowed sanctuary. This gurney is no longer an operating table but rather an altar of sacrifice. This precious soul dying for my freedom is more than just a soldier. He is an offering, passing through the fire for freedom. Receive him, for no greater love, has any man than he that lays down his life for a friend." No, the pathetic enemy whose trembling legs cannot support his cowardly heart using roadside bombs that kill without facing his foe did not get the best of this soldier's sacrifice... God did, and God received home the best of the best for the cause of human dignity in liberty. Freedom is not free.

The Black Hawks were standing by with engines screaming and blades turning while we ducked and ran for the helicopter. Then it was off to Tikrit, and the Sunni Triangle with a heart determined to make a difference in the hearts and minds of every soldier who would cross my path.

I opened the ministry in Iraq with church services in Saddam's palaces! Four of them! In each, I shared God's love and the hope in Christ with the troops. I slept in Saddam's beds and sat on his thrones! At every stop, we lifted the name of Jesus and watched hope and renewal of spirit give smiles back to the battle-hardened soldiers. Laughter filled the echoing chambers of the palaces where random murders once took place. To hear the prayers of the soldiers was heartwarming. To see tears in a commander's eyes at the sight of his troops' new strength, and to personally contribute to their hope of survival emotionally as well as physically, was why God sent me there!

Network television crews followed me to some locations in the safer parts of Baghdad and recorded my presentation at the Martyrs Monument built for the war dead in the war between Iraq and Iran. It was there that I ministered to 800 troops and the Spirit of the Lord was so real. We wept and laughed and celebrated the love of God and the newfound freedom for the people of Iraq. Make no mistake, the troops knew exactly why they were there doing that dangerous job. It was not just for America's security but for the sake of the people of Iraq as well.

It was in Balad that I was given the open door for ministry to some precious Iraqi children. They were injured in an attack on our troops and were hospitalized in the American mobile hospital that had all the necessary equipment to save lives. The kids were frightened at first, but with a little loving attention and teaching them to "high five," they were laughing in no time. The same hospital that held these children and our injured troops also had in some rooms the enemy who was injured by return fire as they ran from our troops. It was so bizarre to see the wounded Americans in the same hospital with the enemy who caused their injuries, receiving the same dedicated and lifesaving treatment as our soldiers.

I ministered to a *Los Angeles Times* reporter who was injured in a car bomb explosion that nearly took his life. He was in a room with several soldiers who were hanging onto life and limbs. He commented over and over about two things. One, he wondered why I would be in Iraq risking my life to be with the troops; and secondly, he said while weeping, "What brave and courageous young troops we have in the military today."

As the tour unfolded throughout Iraq, I was constantly complimented by the leadership for getting out of the safe and secure areas (if there is such a thing) and visiting the troops in the FOBs (Forward Operating Bases). Those are dangerous places. But it was in those remote and unsecured areas where mortars are incoming constantly that I found my heart.

Returning to Baghdad, my assistant asked the Black Hawk pilot if we could ride with the doors of the helicopter open. "Sure," the pilot replied, "make sure your belts are fastened." We double-cinched the belts, and up we went. My seat was on the back row, second from the right, facing forward, and the others were facing the rear of the aircraft. The open door idea was about to be a new war experience for me. I didn't know that the seat I had selected was known affectionately as the snot seat! The wind from the giant oversized blade blew wind in the door, hitting the second from the right rear seat at 100 miles per hour! The wind was horrific! It literally lifted my helmet up off my head, and my hairpiece was sliding out from under it! My right ear, which everybody knows is artificial and removable, did just that. . . it removed! It blew off of my head, and I caught it in midair just as it was headed for the open door! With my ear in one hand, my hair in the other, I did a double-twisted, cross-handed, full-extension finger snatch-and-grab my glasses! The last time my ear and hair were blown off was in Vietnam! All I could think was, "Oh Lord, not again!" My eyes watered, and my nose ran, and I realized why they call it the snot seat!!

I've often had people ask me, "In the light of your success and access to the world through television, high school assemblies, military academics, books, and movies – with all of the notoriety and opportunities brought to you by your injury, you'd go through all of that in Vietnam again, wouldn't you?" For years my response was contained in my own spirit, but I really wanted to slap them and say, "I didn't want to do this the first time, much less do it again." But things have a way of changing with time. Time may not heal all wounds, but it at least heals most of them. One of the last wounds of my life to be healed has been dealing with the ultimate value placed on my personal injury. Would I do it again? It's an awesome question. Believe it or not, some people do go through repeated periods of suffering, a duplication that is unimaginable. To have the privilege of praying with the soldier dying in Baghdad, to know that the last words he heard me say were "Thank you," and the first words he would hear following that were "Welcome home," from the throne of God, has brought about a view, through healing not possible earlier. Would I do it again? Yes, I would. I would do it again and again and again if that's what it took to maximize the value of my personal experience and to say "thank you" for the ultimate sacrifice of those who give their lives in battle.

Chapter 21

Ministry Today

And may the Lord make you increase and abound in love to one Another and to all, just as we do to you. 1 Thessalonians 3:12

God has opened incredible doors for me to share the message of the Gospel of Jesus. What began in a small church with a scared and scarred man in a hospital robe refusing to let the enemy reign over the fate of his life has now spread around the globe. When He gave the responsibility to minister to veterans, He helped provide a way to touch every area of their lives. We started in Vietnam, but we serve all vets to help them heal in all ways. We have programs for them at our ranches in Texas and Colorado addressing PTSD, marriage strengthening, and freedom from war's lasting pain and effects.

I have reaped favor from my faithfulness in many ways: As told earlier, after the phosphorus grenade blast, I immediately rolled into the river, attempting to extinguish the flames. Surfacing still on fire, I looked into the heavens, screamed, "God, I still believe in You," and thrust my left fist straight up. Those poignant words launched a God-ordained anointing of my life and ministry that continues today in seventy countries. From English-speaking K-12 schools opened in Vietnam to undertakings in Africa, India, and beyond, the Roever worldwide ministry has faithfully spread the "Good News Gospel" of Jesus Christ as our Lord and Savior.

We have been able to watch as God has provided materials that disciple believers so they can enjoy the life God planned for them. We continually translate the materials into different languages and have distributed them in thirty-seven countries. Brenda knew we needed to reach the children, and we have been able to impact the coming generations in countries where most people would have told us we would never be able to reach.

God has made connections with other believers, other ministries, and other non-profits around the globe to make His work possible for us. He has even used unexpected, comical occurrences to move hearts to Jesus. Once, a particularly amusing scenario unfolded in Jamaica at a large outdoor gathering. The weather was muggy, hot, and humid, and I was sweating profusely. I was preaching when my artificial ear fell off and landed on my right shoulder. I couldn't feel it, so I didn't know it had happened. Suddenly, the crowds looked astonished and gasped, so I knew something was wrong.

The first thing I did was check my fly. That was not something I would leave to chance. Then I looked down and saw my ear lying on my shoulder. I grabbed it and stuck it back on my head. The people didn't know it was an artificial ear. They thought they had just witnessed a miraculous healing. There was an immediate reaction with a great deal of praising and worshipping God. They all got saved! I didn't stop and explain that I had an artificial ear. If I had done that, they would have all thought I was a fake preacher and run me out of town. I decided that God could use that to win them over to Jesus, so I prayed with them to receive the Lord.

I've learned to laugh, take everything in stride, and let God work in the midst of whatever I am going through. It has never been about me. It is always about Jesus in me. While there were many spontaneous experiences, everyone who works with me in the ministry diligently prepares and plans for what God is doing through us all.

Chapter 22

Ministry Messages

Come and hear, all you who fear God, And I will declare what
He has done for my soul. Psalm 66:16

My father's admonition to always have a message ready is still a guiding principle in my ministry to this day. The places and the people have changed over time, but the Word of God never has. Holy Spirit gives me fresh words and illustrations of lessons before each engagement. Spirit-filled believers have a close connection that allows for constant communication.

For me, one of the most amazing Scriptures is what we are told about the text of the Bible. It is not some ancient, dust-covered book; it is the living Word of God. Hebrews 4:12-13 describes it this way, *For the word of God is living and powerful, and sharper than any two-edged sword, piercing even to the division of soul and spirit, and of joints and marrow, and is a discerner of the thoughts and intents of the heart. And there is no creature hidden from His sight, but all things are naked and open to the eyes of Him to whom we must give account.*

Because the Word is alive and powerful and God sees all creatures, He can use Scriptures to pierce the heart and win the souls of anyone He has placed on our path. There also are powerful anecdotal stories I frequently share with everyone as I travel worldwide in my ministry. These are two messages that God has given me to use to move hearts powerfully.

A Rosie Day

Each morning at Brooke Army Medical Center, I had an 8:30 appointment with hell. Officially it was called debridement, but that term is far too mild to describe adequately what took place. Everyone with me on Death Row called it hell. The impending appointment was heralded by the gurney's squeaking wheels used to transport us down a long hallway. My dread increased with every new squeak. The tank used was stainless steel in the shape of a cross so that you could lay flat with your arms outstretched. It was filled with an antibacterial saline solution at just the right level to submerge our entire body leaving only our face above the surface.

The initial entry into the tank caused stinging and burning. It was much like laying down on a scorching hot surface while fire ants sting you all over your body. It was good for us because it helped eliminate dead skin and restore saline to healthy skin. However, it was incredibly hard on our mental and emotional sense of well-being while going through it. After we soaked for a while, the debridement began in earnest. The nurses pulled and cut away the dying skin, which always hurt. Watching pieces of yourself being cut off your body and discarded was difficult.

When what remained of my nose was pulled on, cut away, and discarded, I experienced deep pain. The ache from the inside overshadowed the physical pain on the outside. The pain was accompanied by the reality that I would be scarred and disfigured for the rest of my life. This hell we visited every day was filled with screams, moans, and other sounds of agony I have no words to describe. We were given morphine before our appointment, but no drugs were strong enough to dull or diminish this pain.

One morning amid this hellish activity, the mind-bending drugs, and overwhelming pain triggered the "fight" response deeply established in my mind when I became a Navy warrior. The nurse working on me, performing the procedures that would help me heal and keep me from dying from gangrene, bent close to me as she was scraping and cutting. She had long hair, and deep inside me, I heard, *"She is trying to kill you!"* I responded in the only way a warrior would. Kill or be killed was ingrained in my very being. I grabbed her hair as best I could, flipped her over, and pushed her head under the water. Instantly five other nurses responded, freed her from my grip, and calmed me down. When I looked at this beautiful soul, drenched in blood-tinged water with pieces of my skin hanging off of her, I was filled with anguish and remorse, realizing I had tried to kill her. "He's had enough," the charge nurse said. Indeed, I honestly had had enough.

The medic loaded me on the gurney with the squeaky wheel, and we slowly rolled down the hall. He got me settled back in bed in Death Row. As he turned to walk away, he said, "Tomorrow morning; we will do this again at 8:30."

I sat up and angrily said, "No, I'm not!"

"Then you'll die," he replied.

"Well, if you are going to do this to me again, don't tell me – surprise me."

Puzzled, the medic returned to me and asked, "Why, what is the difference?"

"I'll be awake all night with multiple anxiety attacks because I'll be dreading tomorrow morning since I will know that at 8:30, you will be coming to take me to hell."

The following day, at the appointed time, I heard the squeaky wheel gurney announcing that the angel of pain was approaching. They rolled it next to my bed but failed to lock the wheels. As they began to transfer me, I fell between the bed and the gurney. I was able to catch myself about halfway down as I fell through the crack.

In that unforeseen situation, my life took a turn that hadn't been as big since I had found out I wasn't a Mexican as I thought I was when I was growing up. It was caused by a man I had never seen before who did things differently than others. He stood at least 6'7" and weighed about 350 pounds. He was made of solid muscle, so when he moved, cannon balls popped up on his chest and shoulders. His arms were massive. He was bald, he was black, and his name was Rosie. That name was tattooed across his arm. He put one arm under my neck, and I knew he was trying to help me. I gave him as much leverage as possible with the best effort I could manage. He lifted me as easily as if I were a feather with his other arm. He turned but didn't place me on the gurney.

For Rosie, there was no need to use a gurney. He carried me down that long corridor to the place called hell. Then he lowered me into that torturous tank. As they started soaking, stripping, and ripping my skin, I watched as he folded his massive arms, stepped back, and leaned against the wall. The morning sun cast a golden hue on his beautiful, ebony skin. I could see tears dripping onto his arms from what looked like rivers of fire running down his sunlit face. Then I noticed his lips were moving. He was praying for me. Rosie was praying for me! Knowing someone was praying for me, knowing that somebody cared, lifted my spirit. At that moment, I decided to hold on to life. Rosie had brought me a gift from God.

At last, they said, "He's had enough." With that statement, Rosie came over and lifted me out of that filthy water. He dried his arms with a terry cloth and gently dabbed my bleeding body. Then turned and carried me back to Death Row. Walking slowly down the hall, he repeatedly said, "You'll be fine, big man, you'll see. You'll be fine." Lowering me onto the mattress and carefully stroking my head, he said again, "You'll be fine, big man, you'll be fine." I looked into his eyes, which seemed to show me a galaxy of twinkling stars, and I felt an overwhelming deep peace.

Who was this Rosie? Was he an angel placed on earth to help me? My soul asked, but the answer was beyond my ability to find it.

Many years later, I finished a message to a large group and began gathering everything to leave the meeting room. A woman approached me and asked, "Are you, Dave?"

"Yes, Ma'am, I am."

"But isn't your full name David?"

"Yes, it is."

"But that's not your first name. Isn't that Milton?"

Now I was taken aback and curious. "Yes, it is. But tell me, who are you, and how do you know me?"

"Oh, I'm the nurse you pulled into the tank twenty years ago."

Apologetically I said, "Oh, I'm so very sorry! Can you ever forgive me for that? It hurt my heart so much that I did that to you; I know you were only doing your job and trying to save my life."

She assured me all was forgiven and expressed her compassion and understanding of what a difficult journey I had.

Then I asked, "Do you remember a guy named Rosie?"

Looking stunned, she answered, "I haven't thought of him for years, but I remember him. He had his name tattooed on his arm."

Then I peppered her with short-answer questions.

"Do you know his real name?"

"No, I don't think I ever heard it."

"When did he come?"

"Well, he came about the time you did."

"When did he leave?"

"Now that you mention it, I guess around the time you did."

I reflected on these answers, which brought a barrage of more questions. Was he an angel of the Lord? My friends think he was since Scripture tells us in Psalm 34:7, *The angel of the Lord encamps all around those who fear Him and delivers them.* Rosie did come and deliver me that day. But aren't all angels covered with white feathers? Do they have tattoos? Is that even allowed?

I hope he wasn't an angel. If he was, then he was just on assignment, doing what his commander told him to do. But if he was a man, he was on a mission doing what he wanted to do, and he didn't care what rank I was, what branch of the service I was in, what color my skin was, or even if I had any. He saw a guy falling through the cracks of life, caught me in the fall, lifted me, and carried me where I could not go on my own. He loved me when I hated myself. He encouraged me when I had no room for encouragement. He spoke words of hope into my life as he carried me.

When we have Jesus Christ inside us, we are called to be a Rosie to somebody today. Pick them up when they are down, take them where they can be healed, and speak words of hope when they are hopeless.

Love them when they have no love. Be Jesus in the flesh. The world is filled with pain and suffering, and people may be close to giving up. Somebody on your life path may be at a point of deciding that ending their life is their only way out of the pain. Show them Jesus. He is the only hope we have for the world today.

Well Digger

As Christians, we know we are all going to heaven; however, we all will pass through some Valleys of Weeping on the way. Psalm 84:5-7 gives us encouragement for those times.

Blessed is the man whose strength is in thee; in whose heart are the ways of them.[6] Who passing through the valley of Baca make it a well; the rain also filleth the pools. They go from strength to strength, every one of them in Zion appeareth before God. Psalm 84: 5-7

Baca, found in this Scripture, means weeping and mourning. My valley of weeping was when a white phosphorus incendiary grenade I was about to throw exploded and severely burned half my face, the top of my head, and the upper portion of my torso. Because white phosphorus sticks to a person's skin as it continues to burn at 5000°, it causes extensive second and third-degree burns. Injuries such as these leave phosphorus in a person's body. Absorption of that chemical usually causes a greater risk of dying since the liver, heart, and kidney are damaged. Many times, it leads to multiple organ failures.

The skin on the right half of my body was burned off, and the left side was used to graft skin onto the injured half. In my valley of weeping, I was horribly burned on one side of my body; on the other, I was being skinned alive. I was literally in a living hell in the valley of Baca. Only hell's minions could have orchestrated that scenario.

Baca is where there is no expectation of reward; there is no credit given for good; pain and suffering push the soul to the brink of despair. In that place, there is no hope to be found. The valley of weeping is where twenty-two veterans each day are when they commit suicide to end the agony of living.

The Word of God found in Psalm 139 assures us that if we ascend into heaven, He is there in that place. Yet it also reminds us that if we make our bed in hell, behold, He is there. He is there in that lonely place to shine the light of hope so we can finally find Him.

When the valley lacks life and hope, we need reminders to look for Him. When I looked into the mirror for the first time, I confirmed how truly devoid of hope my life was. The love of my wife and family and the concern and care of others taking care of me helped me find hope once more.

Most theologians agree that David wrote Psalm 84 at a difficult time in his life. He knew how it felt to cross a place where life, sustenance, and hope couldn't be found. His heart was moved as he and his men crossed a desert littered with dried bones of those who couldn't make it through. He gave orders to his men to dig wells. "Change what you can," David must have heard from God. He had his men dig wells. Wells to give hope, encouragement, and life were then left to help sustain the lives of all who would follow them.

David knew that God had blessed and strengthened him, so he made it through the incredibly hard times of life. David also knew that God blesses His people so they can be a blessing to others. If God has blessed you as you fought through the hard times of life, it wasn't just for you because you are special to God. You are special to God, but he also wants to use you to bless others. When God saved my life and brought me back from the edge of destruction, he used other people who knew Him and the living water that He poured into their lives.

I can't know what you are going through now or how you feel. When it hurts the most, you need to lean on Jesus the most. The water of life will bring you through the valley; you will be better for it and know Him in a way you never have before.

I know what it is like to be thrust into the valley of weeping and what it is like to drink from the well that gave me my hope. Filled and refreshed by Him through His children who were placed around me, He filled me with a passion for taking the comfort and the hope I had been given and sharing it with a lost and hurting world: what a blessed mission and a glorious privilege this is.

We must dig wells for others coming through the valley after us. We must be willing to share our experience, strength, and hope while walking through hard things and low, dark places. Please don't miss the mission He has for you. I almost did. When I looked in that mirror, I never thought God could ever possibly use someone who looked like me. Don't rule yourself out. If Jesus thought you were worth saving, He knew there was a purpose for you in his kingdom. Perception of the outer man will change when people see what is in your inner soul.

When we bought our homestead property in Fort Worth, nothing was on it; it was utterly unimproved. There were no utilities at all. I moved an airstream travel trailer onto the property, and we lived in it for nine years.

When we finally were ready to build a house, I called a well-digging service so that we could have water in the house. I opened the Yellow Pages to well-digging services, chose the first name listed there, and called Allred Well Digging. After a couple of rings, the phone was answered with a gruff, slightly irritated, "What?"

I timidly asked, "Is this Allred Well Digging?"

"Yes!" came the short answer.

"Is Mr. Allred there?"

"Yes."

"Are you, by chance, Mr. Allred?"

"Yes"

"I need a well," I responded with what I thought was the beginning of my explanation about what I needed.

The short response was, "Where," which showed me that no explanation was needed. I gave him my address.

"When?"

"Today?"

"Okay."

The phone line then went dead.

I waited four hours by the blacktop road on the dirt lane on my property. Finally, a rusted old white pickup drove up. There was so much rust I could barely make out the now faded name Allred Well Digging Services painted on it. I watched as an old man bounced his way up the lane with buckets falling off the dilapidated vehicle, and it prompted me to think, *"Jed Clampett has come to dig my well."* He gradually rolled to a stop since his brakes were in the same rickety condition as the old truck.

"Are you Mister Allred? Thank you so much for coming." My enthusiastic greeting was mostly because he had shown up.

"Where do you want the well?"

"So much for small talk," I thought. "I don't know where I want the well. Can't you tell me that? Do you have a divining rod or something?" My hope of finding a satisfactory well digger was quickly fading.

"Where are you going to build a house?"

I showed him, and he responded, "Why don't we drill the well by where you want the house." This common-sense question reassured me somewhat.

He began to pull long pipes out from under the truck. They were the drill stems he would use to build the well. He began to push the pipe down through the caliche soil, which popped and cracked as it gave way to the pipe. I thought he wouldn't go more than six feet before it would break. The first one was pushed in then he began to add more pipe; finally, after drilling down one hundred twenty-five feet, he stopped. That is when he hit the third level of the Trinity River Aquafer. He poured some of it into a little tin cup and handed it to me. It was so cold that it instantly produced condensation on the outside of the cup. When I took a drink, I knew it was the best water I had ever tasted. Fifty years later, I still drink that water. That well has never run dry and continually brings water up from below.

When the well-digger came that day, I saw only the outside of him. He was an old man wearing battered boots coated in layers of dirt. He was dressed in nasty clothes bearing mud from his last well. I looked at his old rusted dilapidated truck, wondering how in the world he could get the job done with that contraption.

When he arrived to drill for water that day, I could have let my critical judgment send him away. However, if I had, I would have missed a blessing that has been an important part of my life for fifty years. Once he let me taste the water, my opinion of him completely changed.

I looked at him and said, "Sir, that is mighty fine equipment you have there. Your boots are perfect for this job. Those overalls you have on make a great uniform for this job."

He grinned sheepishly and said, "Thank you so much."

I discovered that nobody cares what you look like when delivering the water. In a thirsty dying world, they just want to drink the cold, free-flowing water of hope.

Occasionally, people comment that the day I was blown up must have been the worst day of my life. I never agree with them. When I was blown up, I learned to lean on Jesus. I journeyed through a long and arduous valley of weeping. Since then, there have been more challenging physical things I have endured. I have had sixty surgeries; the last ten have been the most painful. I could not have made it without Jesus. He never left me, forsake me, nor ever let me give up. He never will. He also wants to be there with you, no matter your circumstances.

Why am I telling these stories about myself? There is only one reason. If there is even one person at the end of their hope, who needs to laugh again and live again, I don't want to miss an opportunity to give them hope. You see, I am a well-digger. When I dig down into my stories and can still laugh and live, I leave some hope for others coming up through that valley of weeping. I fell into the water on that river when I was set on fire. When I surfaced, my first words were, "God, I still believe in you!"

I hadn't walked away from my belief in Jesus for the eight months of my deployment. The world around me offered plenty of opportunities to turn away from Him into sin. Even when I was taunted and ridiculed, I knew the sweet life Jesus offered me would always be what I wanted.

Two of us from my unit were severely injured by that grenade. I was told the other man had died. He also had been told that I had died. Thirteen years later, he heard my voice on a radio show and called in, asking, "Is this Preacher Man?"

I immediately recognized his voice and asked, "Is this Pervert Number One?" I gave him my office number, and we spoke on the phone after the show. Both of us were surprised that the other was still alive.

I told him I was speaking at a crusade that night and asked if he would come. He said he would. There were thousands of people that night, so I asked him to come early. As the time to begin was approaching, I was about to give up on him coming when an usher walked up with an envelope with my name on it. Inside there was no note, just a .50-caliber live round in it. That was message enough; I knew he was there. It was a .50-caliber shell that devastated his life when it blew off his leg and shredded his hand to pieces.

Before I spoke that evening, I asked the crowd to indulge me. I explained there was a man who served with me and was injured simultaneously, and I wanted to see if he was there.

I asked my question, "Is Mickey Block here?" I saw him rise, place his crutches under his arm, then make his way to the front on his one leg. Coming down the sloped walkway, he almost lost control and fell. I rushed to meet him at the front. We held each other for a long time, letting that hug convey all the words buried in our hearts. Then we began to talk to Jesus. That night, he gave his life to Jesus, who led him onto the path He had planned for him. He went on to become an evangelist, ultimately speaking all over the world.

He had been on the top bunk when we were deployed. I didn't try to win him to Jesus. In fact, I didn't have the love in my heart for him I should have. I didn't know he was watching the way I lived my life. He saw a life his soul desperately wanted. He drank from the well I dug when I followed the ways of Jesus against all the pressure of the world.

God created us all to be well diggers to provide living water, bringing hope to all those around us who are walking through the valley of weeping.

***

Those messages and many others go into church pulpits and are used wherever God opens doors. Amazing testimonies come in after meetings we hold. God works through His people to save and deliver and bring His children home.

He also uses the messages He gives me to encourage those on my path who need to step forward into His calling in their lives. The first time was in my ministry's very early stage when I went to Vietnam to bring the gospel to that country. I knew they had a desperate need for that message. There was no way I could have known at the time that God was planning to touch a certain young man's life and then use him to touch so many others as he came to work alongside me in our ministry. God has a wonderful plan and purpose for every one of His children.

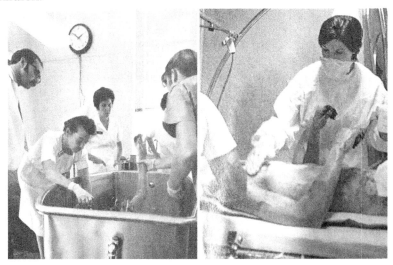

Chapter 23

Dan Dang's Story

Go therefore and make disciples of all the nations, baptizing them in the name of the Father and of the Son and of the Holy Spirit. Matthew 28:19

In 1974 when I first met Dave Roever in Da Nang, South Vietnam, I was a fifteen-year-old boy who had grown up surrounded by war. Often, history books record the dates, facts, and numbers of war but don't portray the impact it has on the lives of the people living through it. In my divided country, the North was fighting the South. My house was about a mile away from a small, highly classified U.S. Army Green Beret and CIA military base, so we were constantly alert for NVA and Viet Cong rocket attacks. When they were fired, they often missed the base and landed close to our house. As the war progressed, we had to run to our underground bunker more frequently when the shelling started. After a particularly intense attack, one morning, I opened my eyes and saw the blue sky where the ceiling of my room had been. The constant shelling had taken off the top of my house. On another occasion, a 122 mm rocket landed in front of my house but did not detonate. When the skirmish ended, the shell was discovered by the Army of Vietnam (ARVN) explosive experts, who could not explain why the shell had not exploded. My dad said, "We know why. I am the pastor of this church, and God protected us."

My father was a pastor who led a Christian Church in Da Nang. He had organized a group of about five hundred students to hear Dave Roever, a Vietnam veteran, bring a message of hope. The night before the assembly, Dave met with my father. When I saw him for the first time, he was still recovering from his injury and was extremely disfigured. I was frightened by his appearance and didn't want to get close to him. Remarkably, he joked around about the way he looked. When he saw several of us standing nearby and staring, obviously frightened, he raised his hands, sprang toward us, and growled like a tiger. We all screamed, and it was all I could do to keep from peeing in my pants. That night I had monster-filled nightmares because of his shocking appearance and playful lunge at us.

The next day at the assembly, my perception of him changed dramatically when he stepped forward to the podium. I was amazed when he held up a bible and began to speak, saying, "The first time I came to your country, I brought an M-16. Now I have come back carrying John 3:16 to tell you about Jesus."

Then he told how the phosphorus grenade had blown up in his hand, burning him severely all over his body. He fell into the river; when he came out of the water, he loudly proclaimed, "God, I still believe in you." From the platform that day, he said the exact words that my heart silently cried out each time one of the rockets flew over us as I watched my country be devastated by war.

Hearing what he had to say, my heart was moved. It was incredible that this man returned to the country where he had been hurt so severely while fighting for my people's freedom. Most men would have hated the country and the people in it. Most men would never have wanted to come back. This man, however, had the guts to get up in front of people looking the way he did and proclaim the Gospel of Jesus. His words lit a fire in me to share the Gospel too.

After the assembly, I went to my dad and told him I wanted to follow in the footsteps of Mr. Dave Roever. Even when I said those words, I never dreamed I would ever come to the United States of America.

Previously, my only dream was to one day become an ARVN general so that I could defend and die for my country. I wasn't interested in becoming a congressman, senator, or other professional. I wanted to plan, prepare and fight to win freedom for my country.

The Vietnamese educational system required every junior high school student to take a proficiency test. If students didn't pass the test, they were conscripted into the military. That generally happened around the age of sixteen. I was almost old enough to begin the path I was certain would lead me to fulfill my dream. I was so focused on becoming an Army general that Vietnam was the only country that interested me. There were no other languages I wanted to learn nor any other countries I wanted to study. The dream was deeply embedded in my heart and mind. However, when I met Dave Roever, my dream changed.

In March of 1975, when the communists captured Da Nang, my dad told me I needed to take my sister and brothers and go to Saigon. I did not want to leave my parents, so I begged him not to make me leave without him and my mother. He explained that we had to go because it would be too dangerous for us to stay. He also strongly felt that he needed to stay behind to care for the ten thousand congregants in his church. I wasn't much more than a boy myself, but at fifteen, I became responsible for the welfare of my fourteen-year-old brother, eight-year-old sister, and four-year-old little brother. In war-ravaged South Vietnam, we completed the dangerous four-hundred-mile trip without any problems. We found my grandpa in Saigon and lived with him temporarily.

The war intensified and brought the collapse of the old regime with it. On April 28th, which happened to be my birthday, my mom and dad arrived in Saigon. Threats of execution had been made, forcing them to leave to survive. Our family began an unexpected odyssey, which we prayed would lead us to freedom and preserve our lives.

We made three different attempts to escape before we finally succeeded. Each trip down the Saigon River to the South China Sea was more harrowing than the last. We had the good favor of having a boat captain who had experience with the Saigon River. Everyone left with nothing more than the clothes on our backs. Fortunately for all of us, my younger brother wore a red tee shirt the day we left. We tore it into strips, so each of us had a red armband to signify we were politically acceptable.

My dad helped with the escape by ensuring the South Vietnam flag painted on the cockpit wall of the boat was covered with white paint. Then we obtained a new flag the North Vietnam Army (NVA) now had on their boats. My dad had the captain fly that flag on our boat's mast. We were still stopped and questioned, but our claim of being pro-regime naval irregulars patrolling the river was believed. The flag flying on our mast, a red tee-shirt, and the work of the Holy Spirit helped us get through. Once out of sight of land and now on the South China Sea, that flag was taken down, and an SOS flag replaced it.

Aboard the riverboat going out to sea, I sadly watched as my war-ravaged country became smaller and farther away. My home, friends, memories, and the only way of life I had ever known were left behind. As the shoreline finally disappeared, my life-long dream of someday being a general who would bravely defend the country and bring freedom to its people also disappeared from my heart. I felt the Holy Spirit's comfort in the void left in my heart. From the depth of my soul, I prayed, "Jesus, I believe in you. I know you are the living God. Please take care of my family. I don't want to die on this ocean. Save us. Oh Lord, save us,"

Our captain's riverboat experience wasn't enough to help him navigate our way once we were in the vast open waters of the ocean. The visa in our possession was for Malaysia, so the captain set our course in that direction. With the all-consuming focus of escaping Vietnam and the communists behind us, our thoughts turned to survival while we were at sea. The fact that none of us aboard that ship knew where or how we would live if we did survive was a consideration that had to be pushed aside for the time being.

We were at sea for twenty-seven days as we traveled from Saigon to Malaysia and then to Singapore. Once we arrived in Singapore, we learned that their government had an agreement with the North Vietnam Army, which required everybody to be returned to Vietnam. Fortunately for us, the American Navy arrived and started sending refugees from Singapore to the Philippines. They gave our boat's captain instructions on navigating to our destination. They explained that he needed to be extremely careful because if he was off by one degree, we could end up in North Vietnam or China. That significantly increased our fear, and we stayed in constant prayer during the voyage.

When we were halfway there, we were rescued by a U.S. Navy escort ship. I was tremendously relieved when I saw the American flag flying on that ship and sensed that, at last, we were bound for freedom. An

American crew member who spoke Vietnamese came aboard our boat and explained that they would escort us to the Philippines. Everyone on our boat cheered wildly.

As I stood on the deck of the small riverboat floating in the shadow of the US ship, I took my first deep breath in days. My eyes were drawn to the bright American flag gently waving above my head, and I had my first smell of freedom. The stars and stripes became a symbol of great importance to me – something I will always be willing to defend against disrespect or dishonor.

Making our way to a new world in the United States was a journey of restored hope, but at times, it seemed overwhelming. After several months in the Philippines, we were relocated to Guam. From there, we settled in Omaha, Nebraska, where I was able to finish high school. Upon graduation, I told my dad I wanted to attend Bible college, but he said I could not do that. He said it with such firmness and finality that I broke down and cried. I was mad at my dad for deciding that for me. I made up my mind that when I got to heaven, and Jesus asked me why I didn't serve Him, I would say, "Because you put me in my dad's family, and he wouldn't let me."

Of course, my dad had his children's best interests at heart. He wanted all of them to be either an engineer or a doctor. My brothers and sister did precisely that; however, it wasn't the path for me. I went to college and enrolled in pre-medicine. I hated it! Then I transferred to the engineering department. I hated it even more! Then I took some business classes and liked those. I switched my degree plan to a business major but hid it from my dad until the last semester. Graduation was quickly approaching when I knew I had to tell him because he would see my diploma. When I finally told him what I had done, he looked seriously at me and said that I was the loser of the family. That was one of the hardest moments of my life, and I was heartbroken.

I didn't speak English when I first arrived in America. When I studied, I struggled through all the material because I had to translate everything I was learning. It took me hours to finish my homework. However, I persevered, graduated with a degree in business, then I got my MBA. Soon after, I started living the American dream. I had a successful career and was making plenty of money. I enjoyed what I was doing. But there was part of my soul that longed to be a pastor.

As I became more successful in my career, I had increasing opportunities. I managed a national electronics store and was very successful. Once the corporate management noticed that, they decided to send me to stores at different locations to help those stores become more successful. When I was told of their decision to move me to different locations, I thought, *"No matter what they say, I am not moving to Texas. It is entirely too hot in the summers."* But God definitely has a sense of humor because I was transferred to a suburb of Fort Worth, Texas, for three months. That company had 7,000 retail stores across the country, and they sent me there! It was 1991, and I didn't know that God was in the process of doing something big in my life.

As the temporary manager of the new retail store, I was at work in my usual way. I helped a customer find a component to complete their sound system. When I went to the cash register to ring up the sale, I asked the usual question, "What is the name on your account?" The reply was far more than usual. "It's the Dave Roever Ministry," came the answer from the customer. Astonished, I stopped, looked at the customer, and said, "I know Dave Roever."

My reply opened up a discussion leading to an amazing discovery. Dave's brother Al had come to the store to buy the piece they needed for their sound system. Incredibly, the system was in their ministry location, across the parking lot from the store I was managing. I told Al the entire story of how I met Dave in Vietnam seventeen years earlier. We arranged for me to meet Dave, which has led to a lifelong association between us.

During my entire journey, my faith in Jesus never wavered. I continued to attend church and serve when and where I could. Once I arrived in Fort Worth, I attended three different revival meetings. At each meeting, I received the same prophetic word. At the first one, I went forward during the altar call. Someone came up to me, put their hand on my shoulder, and said, "God's not done with you yet. Anything He has promised that will come from Him will be fulfilled." I had no idea what that could mean, so afterward, I returned to my church and continued serving. My dream of becoming a pastor had been stifled so many times in my soul that this word did not awaken it.

I had become a volunteer for Dave Roever and attended what he called a "Family Reunion" meeting for veterans. About seventy people were attending, and at the end, he called people forward for prayer. A Vietnam veteran approached me, put his arm around my shoulder, and said, "God's not done with you yet. Anything He has promised that will come from Him will be fulfilled." That sent a shockwave into my heart. The exact words had been spoken over me once again. It was such a moving moment that I whispered aloud the words that had been buried in my heart. "I want to follow in Dave's footsteps to bring the gospel." God took the scales off my eyes so I could see all the ways He had directed me to this point. I began to see the sacred symbols He had placed on my path. The red armbands seemed like the blood of Christ. Our release came on the third day, just as Jesus's resurrection had. The SOS flag our boat flew came to be seen by me as save, oh save.

That fall, I went to another revival, and the exact words were spoken over me. There was no denying that God was calling me into ministry. In 2004 after much prayer, planning, and preparation, I surrendered everything in my life and went to work for Dave Roever full time. I had finally taken that first step in his footsteps.

I didn't know what I would do yet, but I thought it was to work with Vietnam veterans. I asked Dave what my job was, and he said, "Your job is to do good and tell the world the Gospel of Jesus." Then he told me that when I needed wisdom, I must go and find someone I knew would direct me on the right path.

Dave was taking Vietnam veterans back to Vietnam so they could receive spiritual healing from the wounds the war had left on their souls. I traveled with him on those trips. While I was there, I worked with the local churches. I began to notice that many people were hearing the Gospel and being saved. However, the churches weren't giving new believers the foundation of the Bible that they needed. I knew the churches needed something so they could build that foundation because, without it, believers would fall away. I didn't know how to get involved in doing this.

I knew I needed the wisdom to find the right path. I turned to Brenda Roever. I went to her office and asked, "Boss, can I have five minutes to talk to you?" She gave me a big smile and said, "Dan, I know your five minutes." Chuckling, she added, "This will probably be two hours, but come on in." In that conversation, she suggested I contact Global University for help. Indeed, after the lengthy session, she said, "Dan, now go change the world. Remember, reach the children. If you win the children's hearts for Jesus, they will change the world."

I began working on teaching and training to bring the Gospel and Discipleship to Vietnam through their churches. Dave told me that compassion leads to conversion, which is what we did in Vietnam. We partnered with *Book of Hope* and began taking it into Vietnam. That book focuses on the four Gospels, which we understood were the only hope for the country. It became the first book by an outsider to receive authorization from the communist government to be brought into Vietnam. Since working with Global University, we have seen God's hand in the work being done through them. It has rapidly grown and now has over 150,000 students worldwide.

After all these years with Dave Roever, I have never lost the joy of serving God. REAP International was formed out of the desire to strengthen the Biblical foundation for believers in Vietnam. Today we are reaching out with compassion to children and adults worldwide. Everything we do is designed to bring people closer to Jesus. Watching Him save, transform and heal people's lives also brings me closer to Him.

Long ago, in Vietnam, I dreamed I would become a general who fought to defend and bring freedom to the people of my country. God showed me that in my position with this ministry, I continually fight to defend all people's rights to have access to the Bible. When we successfully tell the Gospel, hearts are won to Jesus, and He sends His Holy Spirit. It is the greatest joy of my life to know the truth found in Second Corinthians Chapter 3, *"Now the Lord is the Spirit; and where the Spirit of the Lord is, there is freedom.* There will always be true freedom in the country of my birth because Jesus has sent His Spirit into the people's hearts. I am blessed to be able to take back territory for God's kingdom through the work of this ministry.

The dream of being a general prepared me to be a leader and to be strong. The great desire for my country to be free has given me the commitment to persevere, plan and produce a great harvest for Jesus in my homeland. He gave me the desire to understand the business principles which have guided our steps as we steward the ministry. It is wonderful that God's ways are not our ways; His are vastly better.

The Family – A Call for Unity

I sensed a widening separation in our relationships when I traveled. In a very real way, I felt the importance of Joshua's stance, "As for me and my household, we will serve the Lord." We were to serve the Lord together.

Chapter 24

The Roevers - Home on the Roam

And these words which I command you today shall be in your heart. You shall teach them diligently to our children, and shall talk of them when you sit in your house, when you walk by the way, when you lie down, and when you rise up.
Deuteronomy 6:6-7

J esus was clear about what His followers would be called to do as He spoke to them just before He ascended into Heaven. The Book of Acts, Chapter One, records His instructions, *"You shall receive power when the Holy Spirit has come upon you, and you shall be witnesses to Me in Jerusalem, and in all Judea and Samaria, and to the end of the earth."*

I was excited about doing just that. Jesus had brought me through something I could not have gone through without Him. I knew He did the things He did for me, but I knew it wasn't just for me. The other servicemen returning from war needed to hear about Jesus, and I was a willing and ready witness to testify about Him.

At the beginning of my ministry, Brenda and I traveled around the country, living in a small car-towed travel trailer. Traveling together was exciting and gave us flexibility in our schedule. As our babies came along, it became a bit more of a challenge. We increased the size of our trailer and, at one point, lived in a bus as we traveled, and it all worked out just fine.

The road trips broadened our children's experiences. They learned how to become friends with other children quickly and how to play in and around different churches. Once, as I was preaching, I noticed Matt crawling around, counting the number of pieces of gum stuck under the chairs. When I saw him decide to see what flavor one piece was, I went over, picked him up, and held him on my lap as I continued preaching.

In 1976, when Matt was school-aged, we decided that it was better for him to have the experience of going to public school. To restrict some traveling, I arranged opportunities to preach close to home. We bought some land in Fort Worth that was just that, land. We pulled our trailer onto the property and established it as our home base.

Matt excitedly started school at Eagle Heights Elementary School. His First-Grade teacher, Mrs. Pendry, was a great teacher who helped launch his love for learning. We met and let her know she had our full support as his teacher. She believed that it was in a child's best interest to be taught to behave well. Several times, the "board of education" was applied to Matt's backside so he could learn that lesson. Our home rule was that if you get into trouble in school, you are in trouble when you get home. He quickly learned the importance of doing the right thing. Kim began school two years after Matt, and they both had great experiences. Our lives were similar to many traveling evangelists; I was gone frequently, primarily on weekends, leaving Brenda and the kids to live at home without me.

Brenda was very frugal in all that she did. I had become accustomed to her bargain-hunting and penny-pinching efforts so we would never waste anything the Lord had given us. She took seriously the ways Proverbs 31 laid out for a good wife. Verse 27 particularly seemed to guide her; *"She watches over the ways of her household."*

One of the most impressive things she did in that regard led to a way for us to build a house that would become our permanent home. Our land was in the middle of a weather phenomenon known as "tornado alley." This area stretches from north Texas across Oklahoma and into Missouri. Springtime always brought those terrible storms which left destruction and debris in their wake. One came through as we were starting the process of building a house. Fortunately, no people were killed in the storm, but it left considerable damage in the area. Brenda heard that it had destroyed some silos near our property. They were so damaged that they could not be repaired; therefore, the owner was tearing them down and discarding them. Now, there are not many people who would have seen this as an answer to her prayers, but Brenda did. She heard "rubble" and translated it as "two by fours." The owner of the silos could not salvage them in the size he needed. However, they would be perfect for our house when cut into the sizes needed to build a house. She asked for them and got a "Yes, ma'am" from the owner since he was glad he wouldn't have to pay someone to carry them away.

Brenda gathered her helpers, including Brother Roop, a carpenter. Then she assigned jobs to everyone, even the kids, and soon lumber was stacked neatly on our property. It was a fantastic project. The construction began, and we all worked together to make this dream come true. On any given day, there was sawing and hammering; Matt and Kim were picking up nails and sawed-off ends of boards, so the area was kept neat, and our hearts were happy as we did this work. I didn't have the full use of my hands, but I wanted to be involved. I figured out how to tape a hammer to my hand so I could participate in building our home. It was no mansion, but it became a place we all loved better than any other house in this world.

We settled into a routine of living in our new house while I traveled as God opened doors. There was no way to know what would happen next in our lives, so we lived with an "every day with Jesus" philosophy. Sometimes it's a small change someone else makes that impacts our lives. That was the case for me. A revolutionary new gadget was developed, which changed my ministry.

With the rise in popularity of the music industry came the development of compact cassette tapes with the ability to reduce noise and produce high-fidelity sound. And, wonder of wonder, it included duplicators capable of quickly producing multiple cassette tape copies. This technology allowed me to record my message, quickly reproduce it on cassette tapes, and sell the tapes at our product table and in other venues. It enlarged my territory allowing far more people to hear about me and the ministry. The opportunities to speak significantly increased, filling me with gratitude and excitement. It also caused me to look at my newly-built home, my loving wife, and my precious children and dread leaving.

Matt finished fifth grade, and Kim completed third grade. It was an excellent experience for them, but I sensed a widening separation in our relationships when I traveled. God had given me the right and responsibility to raise my children in the way they should go. It is the greatest honor He has ever given me.

After praying together and discussing what was best for the family, Brenda and I decided to withdraw the children from public school and establish their homeschooling on the road. She excitedly prepared to teach both children while we traveled. She was a brilliant woman who had excelled in school, so she was enthusiastic about sharing in this part of our children's lives.

It proved to be one of the best decisions we made. Brenda established the love of learning in our children and always encouraged them to learn more and do their best. She created a lifestyle of learning. Her history lessons were often scheduled around our different geographical locations. For example, her lesson about the Civil War included studying the Gettysburg Address while we were in Pennsylvania. We spent time in The Gettysburg National Cemetery in a very hands-on learning environment. Matt and Kim could relate and understand much more because of how Brenda taught them. They excelled in their studies and enjoyed learning together.

In a very real way, I felt the importance of Joshua's stance, *"As for me and my household, we will serve the Lord."* We were to serve the Lord together. "Together" was the over-arching description of our life on the road. We were never more than a few feet away from each other. The shared experiences brought our family closer than we could have ever been before we decided to live this way.

Every one of us had assigned jobs. I expected all of us to do our jobs well. The Word of God makes it clear why we were to do our work that way. I taught the children to live by a verse I held dear. In the third chapter of Colossians, we find out why we live that way. *"And whatever you do, do it heartily, as to the Lord and not to men, knowing that from the Lord you will receive the reward of the inheritance; for you serve the Lord Christ."*

Brenda assigned Kim chores to work alongside her in all she did for the ministry. I assigned Matt various age-appropriate chores. At one time, he helped make the cassette tapes to sell on the product table. He could make ten to fifteen copies while working with the master duplicator that made the tapes. He would carefully place the recordings in the cases, ensuring the labels were lined up and looked professional.

He also had the job of washing the bus. Our bus was our ministry's first impression as we arrived at the next church or meeting place. Since we were working for Jesus, it was essential to keep it looking good. He worked hard at it and didn't complain, except when the temperature was around freezing when we got off the road. Washing a bus in thirty-two-degree weather is not enjoyable.

The outward appearance was not as important as what people would be able to see in our hearts. We must genuinely interact with everyone we meet the way Jesus would have. I believed that if we were wearing His name, people should be able to see Him in us.

In the early days, there was a great deal of unrest in the United States. Civil Rights were very much on people's minds. We became kingdom children when we received Jesus as our savior. However, He wants us to be in the world so we can take His message and love with us everywhere we go. His message we proclaim by how we live is always louder than the message pastors proclaim from platforms. Brenda modeled His love in all she did.

I invited Reggie Dabbs, a powerful speaker who loved the Lord, to share his message during one of the Sunday meetings I led. When it was over, Brenda walked with him back to the product table so he could talk to people wanting to meet him. When they got there, a woman came up to him and said, "You just need to know, you speak so well for a black boy!" Dismayed at what the woman said, Brenda intercepted the conversation, looked the woman in the eyes, and said, "You just need to know, I was watching you during praise and worship. You clapped so well for a white girl." Then, to punctuate the meaning behind the words, she turned and said, "Come on, Reggie, let's go." Reggie looking at her with deep gratitude as they walked away, said, "Thank you so much! You fought for my skin color like most people wouldn't do."

These travels also brought other opportunities for us. We took advantage of everything available in the surrounding area or on our way to the next place. We had great adventures that included hunting, fishing, skiing, motorcycle riding, boating, and many more. Our lives included nearby "mini-vacations," so we didn't have to adjust our schedules or make long trips to get to a vacation site. We were able to include them in our daily lives.

Our children gained confidence in new and different experiences because they lived in new and different experiences all the time. They never meet a stranger and feel at ease in new places. God will always give us exceedingly, abundantly more than we can even imagine or ask. He proved that to us as we put Him first.

Brenda and I were discipled in God's ways when we were raised. Having our children was a blessing; they brought us more laughter and fun times than anything else in our lives. We agreed, though, that they must be discipled so they could live meaningful, happy lives. Children raised as disciples need far less discipline than children who are not, but some discipline is always required. Sometimes parents consider it harsh to discipline when truthfully, it prevents future consequences that may prove far more difficult.

When Kim was a little girl, Brenda taught her to be frugal and respect others. When Brenda cuddled or hugged Kim, she would always take a deep breath and tell her mom how good she smelled. She was a smart little girl, and once, she watched Brenda apply Oil of Olay® after bathing before she dressed. Once, the desire to smell like her mom overtook the little girl. She waited until Brenda was in the other room, quickly went to the coveted jar of cream, and rubbed handfuls of it all over her little face, body, then down her arms and legs. She felt pretty proud of herself until Brenda walked back into the room. The look on her mom's face let her know a lesson was coming. She got a paddling that day because she had been so wasteful and had taken something that belonged to someone else without permission. The punishment was not done in anger but with gentleness and an explanation about why that was not a good way to act.

One day, Matt and Kim argued over some unimportant issue between them. Matt pushed Kim, who fell into the wall and then, theatrically, lay on the floor crying. Brenda came rushing in and swatted Kim. "Yes!" Matt shouted gladly. He was happy he wasn't the one getting into trouble.

However, his mom reached for the fly swatter and came after him. She didn't hurt him; she used the swatter to punctuate that playing too rough was not allowed. In response, Matt gave a little laugh with a grin that was disrespectful. Immediately he knew the situation was not going to end well for him. He received the hand of education applied to the seat of his learning to help him remember the rule.

Our children were taught and trained to make good decisions. When Kim was sixteen, Brenda taught her how to drive a car. They spent hours with Kim behind the wheel and her mom as her instructor. When she had mastered the skill and gained some confidence in her ability as a good driver, they went to the Texas DPS, where Kim easily passed her test and got her license.

Not long after, as any teenager would, she asked to use the car to take her friend with her to Hulen Mall to shop for a couple of hours. Brenda felt confident that she could handle that and gave her the keys. The two girls spent hours going from store to store, looking at and trying on clothes, laughing, and enjoying their day. Then they decided to go to a nearby restaurant for supper. Finally, Kim dropped her friend off at her house and drove home.

Those same hours had ticked off far more slowly on Brenda's clock. She trusted her daughter, but as most mothers do, she became concerned when she was gone far longer than expected. She knew there were payphones throughout the mall, yet she never got a call. This was in the pre-cellphone era when parents didn't have the reassurance gained by tracking their children's whereabouts. Her mother's heart was more worried that something terrible had happened to this precious child than she was that her daughter had done anything wrong.

When Kim turned the car down the driveway, her headlights illuminated her mother standing there waiting. Taken aback, she was silent as she opened the car door and tried to gauge her mother's thoughts by searching her face. Seeing no emotions there came as no surprise. The verbal exchange that night was short. Brenda simply held out her hand, palm up, and said, "Hand me the keys. You will not be allowed to drive again until I am sure that you are mature enough to check in with me when you stay longer than we talked about. Relationships are built on what your actions say. Your actions need to mature."

After a moment to consider what had been said to her, Kim's reply was simply, "Yes, ma'am." It was a long month, and she had ample time to understand the importance of communicating with her mother before she got the privilege of using the car returned to her.

As parents, we also wanted to make sure our children learned skills and developed all their God-given talents. Kim was taught how to sing and grew to love praising and worshipping the Lord. We also let them participate in organized sports as much as we could. Matt frequently was able to play in summer ball programs, although he didn't get to play in high school. He had a natural ability and excelled in baseball.

When Matt turned eighteen, he tried out for professional teams. We were thrilled for him when he made the Mud Hens minor league team. It was quite an accomplishment, particularly since he had none of the other players' high school experiences. Brenda was his teacher, but she was also a guidance counselor as he considered his next steps in life.

She sat with him, genuinely sharing his excitement, but then asked a simple question, "Matt if you take this opportunity and you get injured, what do you have that you can fall back on?" As she discussed the decision with him, he saw the wisdom of pursuing an opportunity to go to college while playing baseball. Soon after, he was accepted at Southeastern Bible College in Lakeland, Florida, where he played baseball on the college team. Because she knew how to guide him, he became the first person in our family to graduate from college; then the first to get a Master's degree, and soon he will have his doctorate.

God entrusted two of His greatest works into our hands to steward. We were blessed by Him when He gave them to us. Our prayer as parents has been that we bless Him by raising them according to His ways. We have watched them become adults who live meaningful lives and love the Lord. It is an extra measure of blessing for them to have become people we not only love but ones we genuinely admire and like.

Above: Standing room only for the first Dave Roever city-wide crusade—August, 1986, Lufkin, Texas. Below: Dave and his family spend most of the year traveling throughout the country in their bus home.

Chapter 25

The Most Wonderful Time of the Year

So all this was done that it might be fulfilled which was spoken by the Lord through the prophet, saying: "Behold, the virgin shall be with child, and bear a Son, and they shall call His name Immanuel," which is translated, "God with us"

Matthew 1:22-23

Some of the greatest times for our family were during the Christmas season. We were submerged in the routine, procedures, and culture of the Brooke Army Medical Center on our third Christmas as husband and wife. Brenda valued Christmas and the celebration that came with it. It simply was not something she was willing to skip. That was not the most memorable Christmas, but she somehow made it extremely special. I wasn't able to give her my usual gift. I loved how she smelled while wearing Chanel No. 5® perfume, so I wrapped up a big bottle every Christmas and put it under the tree for her. She pretended she couldn't possibly guess what I had gotten her every year. Her antics made both of us laugh.

I was in a coma in the hospital in Japan following my injury. A nurse wearing Chanel No 5® came in to take care of me. That scent is so powerfully connected in my brain to Brenda that it brought me out of the coma. Not aware of where I was or what I was going through, I reached up with my bandaged hands, put them around the back of the nurse's neck, and pulled her down. I was trying to kiss her because I thought she was Brenda. She said, "Whoa, sailor, you aren't ready for that!" and quickly left my room.

No matter where we lived or were, Brenda created the greatest joy in our home around celebrating Jesus' birth. The tradition of happy, silly, joy-filled activities shared by family, friends, and sometimes people we didn't even know began with her mother. Because this family was very reserved and rarely expressed their feelings, the outward expression of heartfelt joy over the birth of their Savior was even more extraordinary.

Brenda's mother's tradition of having a big celebration at Christmas began when Brenda was a small child. It expanded exponentially as the children grew and began to include the extended family of siblings, spouses, and anyone needing a place to belong for a holiday. By the time our children got older, it had grown so large that I made room in my barn for the festivities. These celebrations had twenty to thirty people who came ready to celebrate.

There was music, many games, special holiday food, and more gifts than you could count. The overriding purpose of these times was to remember that no matter what else anyone had in life, Jesus Christ had given a gift to each of them that was a gift for all eternity. That gift would just keep getting more precious every year. It was as if Brenda provided so much fun that people could store up the joy of their salvation to get them through whatever the new year might bring.

After her mom died, we didn't have the big party in the barn anymore because it wouldn't have been the same without her. Our celebrations were with our kids in our house, but there was no lack of fun, games, and surprises planned by Brenda. One year, in the tradition of young Texas boys' presents, Matt received a BB gun and a Bible. He was only five years old then, but he has always said both were exactly what he wanted. She would tape dollar bills to the floor, making a path to each child's present. She would hide money in the most surprising places.

Once a $100 bill was tucked up into boxes of life-saver candy. The family had many gifts to open that day, and only one person paid attention to their Christmas box of life-saver candies. When that $100 bill was finally discovered, the rest of the family excitedly went to find theirs. They all dug through the Christmas wrapping paper that had filled a trash bag and was now in the dumpster. Dumpster diving was unplanned, but it was a big hit based on the amount of laughter and hilarious antics that Christmas.

When the laughter and fun died down, the true meaning of Christmas was brought up. While the outward celebration created traditions that our children practice today, the inward joy that came from knowing that everyone had been given the greatest gift of all was the only lasting gift. The salvation that comes only through faith in Jesus will be with our children and their children for generations. There is no greater joy than knowing that.

As the grandkids got older, our children celebrated at their own houses, and Brenda and I started celebrating Christmas with just the two of us. Our last Christmas together was in 2020. She gave me a banana-yellow Corvette with black wheels. It was beautiful, about three inches long, and had a little electric motor with remote control. She got a little red Mustang for herself. We had so much fun racing them around the house.

Two weeks later, I was utterly stunned when there was a banana-yellow 2006 Corvette with black wheels that would run like a scalded dog sitting in my driveway. It is my favorite car in the world, and I will never get rid of it. It took Brenda years to save up the money to buy that car. It is the best *thing* I have ever been given; I will drive it for as long as possible. Whether large or small, over the years, she filled all our homes with joy. She gave everyone many gifts, ranging from silly to breathtaking. However, none of those activities or gifts of "things" caused us to lose the main focus of Christmas.

She had her first Heavenly celebration of the Savior's birth in 2021. What incredible joy must have filled her heavenly mansion! That will be my focus for Christmas from now on. There will be no fun, games, or gifts. The only way I will be able to get through Christmas is by focusing on Heaven. Because of Christmas, I won't give up; I will press on with the mission He has given me. A life without Christ would be as empty and broken as my home and heart feel today. Knowing that she is with Him in Heaven and that one day I will be there with her again renews my desire to share the gospel wherever possible. I cannot live without Christ, and I want to tell others that they don't have to, either!

CHAPTER 26

You Can't Kill
a Christian

Christ will be magnified in my body, whether by life or by death. For to me, to live is Christ, and to die is gain. Philippians 1:20-21

O ur country has been under a terrible attack during the recent pandemic. Brenda's brother, Will, was infected with COVID-19 and passed away. As with so many others, it was an unexpected, sudden loss. We went to be with her family and then attended his funeral. It was comforting to celebrate having him in our lives, but unfortunately, we returned home with more than comfort.

Brenda and I contracted the virus within a few days of returning home. At first, the symptoms were mild, but we quickly progressed from "not bad" to "fairly bad." However, I started to recover but could see that Brenda was not getting better. While we were sick, an unprecedented freeze slowly moved across the state of Texas. The first arctic blast took temperatures down to nine degrees Fahrenheit and then moved them lower for over a week. We were isolated from most of our family and friends because of ice and snow and the CDC's requirement to quarantine anyone with the virus.

Brenda was texting health updates to our family, yet she was also trying to keep them from worrying. She sent Matt texts telling him she was getting better and would be fine soon. She often put others first. Unfortunately, she did not start recovering and then took a definite turn for the worse. It became apparent that she needed further medical help. When the ambulance arrived at our house, they hurriedly loaded her and drove away.

There is no lonelier nor more helpless feeling in the world than watching the one person you love more than any others being taken away and knowing you can't go with her. I asked people close to me to come to my home, and we began praying. We prayed from a place of belief that God would help and heal her. Matt was surprised when he got the call about her condition that night since Brenda hadn't prepared him for how bad the virus had gotten. The icy roads prevented him from coming over to be with me. While we talked on the phone, we prayed together. Next, he got on social media to send out a call to pray to all our prayer warrior friends. That connection grew as people posted and reposted the prayer request. Knowing the prayers were being lifted from so many true believers was reassuring.

We prayed hard. We prayed Scripture. We prayed in the Spirit. We prayed with tears. We prayed until I couldn't stay there and pray any longer. I finally reached the place where I knew I must see my beloved.

The hospital rules were stringent and strictly enforced. I didn't care at that point. I had to see Brenda. I had no idea where she was other than the name of the hospital where they said they had taken her. I grabbed my keys and left with the intention that nothing would stop me from being with her.

I drove too fast, and God must have been with me during this trip as He always had been throughout my life. Pulling into the driveway closest to the hospital doors, I saw a workman who had just gotten off his shift walking out. I lowered my window and yelled at him. "My wife is here. I have to see her. I have to see Brenda." I'm sure my agitated state came clearly across with those words. Using a reassuring voice, he said, "Sir, just park anywhere you want." He motioned toward the adjacent parking lot.

Screeching to a halt in the first open spot in that lot, I threw open my door, intending to take off toward the entry doors. After my first step, I realized a woman was standing in the dark parking lot. She was no more than twenty feet from my door, and I realized I knew her. How God coordinated this reunion is nothing short of a miracle.

She was a nurse we knew. As soon as she saw me, she said, "Dave, I've been monitoring your wife's condition. It is not good, and this won't end the way you want it. I wish I could help, but all I can do is get you through to her room so you can see her." She knew I needed to be prepared for what I was about to face. True to her word, she got me to the area where Brenda was located.

At first, the nurses on that floor didn't think I could be there, but they realized the great need in my heart and finally relented. They decided it could be arranged under the heading of a "compassion visit," something not many got to do. They suited me up in what looked like a hazmat suit on steroids. When I went in, I was sure Brenda couldn't tell it was me.

I walked close to her and said, "It's me; it's your long-lost husband." She turned, looked me in the eyes, and her face lit up. I could see her beauty. This disease was attacking her body and doing awful things to her, but it couldn't touch her beauty. My heart leaped within me just the way I always responded to her. Then she reached out and touched my hand. It is difficult to find the words to describe the level of the electric shock that went through my body when I felt her touch. With it came joy and a deep sense of connection. It is perhaps what we will feel when we get to heaven, and Jesus reaches out to us with his loving hands.

That day in her hospital room, I was strengthened for what was ahead. God had given me the powerful sense that it was time for me to go to Brenda. God placed me in the parking lot at precisely the same time the nurse walked by my parking space because that was part of His plan. She opened the way for me to get to Brenda's side to connect with her while she could still communicate. That day, with our roles reversed, I stood by her hospital bedside, murmured her sweet nickname, "Benny Lou," and told her how much I loved her. She held my hand and whispered, "Oh, Davey, I love you so much."

Those would be the last words she spoke to me on earth. Soon after she said them, the virus ravaged her body, and her condition began to fail. I couldn't grasp the reality of what the doctors were telling me. They sent me out of the hospital that night with solid reassurance that they would do everything possible to save her. I was numb and felt like

I was sleepwalking as I returned home. Over the next few days, the roads cleared, so Matt and Kim were with me. They were constant sources of help by talking to the nurses to have all the updates and dealing with the hospital's financial details to process Brenda's account.

The prayers continued fervently. I couldn't focus on anything except interceding for my sweet wife. The prayer network created on social media soon grew to over thirty thousand people. Thousands of comforting and confirming comments were posted. It helped us to know that people weren't just praying for her; they also believed she would be healed. We all were holding tightly to that belief.

I had fallen into a restless sleep when Matt entered the bedroom at 2:14 a.m. Gently shaking my shoulder, he said, "Dad, they called and said we need to get down there right now." I was instantly awake, and we immediately began the longest journey I had ever taken. I was frantic to get to her, yet I feared what they might tell us.

We saw them working hard to help Brenda when we walked into the hospital room. The nurse told us she had "coded," but they weren't giving up. Seeing her in such a poor condition was very hard on us all. The nurse took us to another room so we wouldn't have to watch what they had to do to her poor body.

We cried out to the Lord in anguish, praying for Him to intervene. In a few moments, the nurse returned to the room where we were waiting and said she had coded again.

This was by far the hardest, most painful moment in my life. It exceeded anything I had gone through on the riverbank in Vietnam. This was happening to my Brenda, who had brought nothing but joy and happiness into my world. The enemy was raining down pain and suffering she didn't deserve, and now, even in trying to save her, the medical staff were causing more pain. It was enough. I looked at the nurse and said, "That's enough. Don't hurt her anymore. Don't break any more of her ribs. Please, let her be."

My heart broke. She was leaving me, but I loved her too much to keep trying to hang on to a body that couldn't hang on anymore. They took Matt, Kim, and me back to her room. As we walked down the hallway, Matt said what we were all thinking in our hearts, *"Lord, it's time for you to show up."* When we got to her room, she was gone.

My grief engulfed and poured forth from me. There are no words to capture its magnitude as it came wave upon wave. The depth of grief over losing someone equals the depth of love you shared. The love we shared had grown ever deeper over the fifty-eight years since I first laid eyes on that sweet girl when she was thirteen. I could not imagine how I would survive without her. In the coming hours, there were moments when I didn't even want to try.

God has graced me with family and friends who love and support me so much that I was able to make it through those first days by clinging to my faith and leaning on those around me. I was in deep pain at first, so much so that I could barely function. As we began to plan how we wanted to celebrate having Brenda in our lives and all that meant to each of us, I began to find a bit of purpose. I still struggled through the fog of grief. Kim, Matt, and I were going through all the memory prompting photos when I was sure I heard Brenda's voice. *"Keep it together; there are things to be done."* It was as if Kim heard it, too, because she said, "We need to mention how strong Mom was, particularly when we were going through hard things. Remember what she would always say?" We all said in unison, "Keep it together; there are things to be done."

It became the focus. We had things to do to be able to honor her. We also had things to do to keep the ministry moving forward. She had worked too hard to build it up for us to stop doing what needed to be done.

The pictures and memories filled the following days as we worked together to openly share our lives with all those coming to honor Brenda. One night when sleep wouldn't come, I sat alone with the many memories of my life with Brenda. I remembered our relationship's early years when I sometimes just knew I would lose her. That was all based on my insecurity because she was so beautiful and special.

Over the years, however, four guys tried to take my wife away from me. I don't blame them for trying, and I am just grateful she stayed with me all those years I had with her.

The first guy was a co-worker she worked with at Allstate Insurance. I was fighting in the jungles of Vietnam for the cause of freedom. He had no respect for that at all. He tried to get her to go out with him even though he knew she was my wife. Later she told me about it. I got even with that guy. I only buy State Farm Insurance.

The second guy was a medic on my ward at Brook Army Medical Center. This man flirted with my wife in my presence. He didn't think I was going to make it through to recovery. One day when he came into my room, I faked dying. He came close and bent down to hear me. When he got close, I bit his ear until he bled. Then I growled at him, saying, "If you touch her, I'll kill you." I can't imagine what I could have done to him while I was in that current state, but he didn't seem to question it. He must have moved off my ward because I never saw him again.

The third one was one of her college professors. He brought her flowers and flirted with her. He knew she was married; that's what the ring on her finger was all about. Then he saw a picture of me. He figured if I survived what I had gone through, I must be too tough to be messed with, so he left her alone.

But the fourth one was different. When he came along, he really did catch her eye. He genuinely loved her, too. He made promises to her that I couldn't keep. He also gave her gifts I could never have given her. He stole her heart, and she ran off with him. I got his name, and I know where he lives. His name is Jesus, and he lives in heaven. He told me that if I'm a good boy, I'll be with her again one day. So, I'm going to be a good boy.

The prayer we lifted to Jesus as we walked to Brenda's hospital room for the last time that day was heard. We said to Him, "Lord, it's time for you to show up." Indeed, it was time. She had finished her work on earth and fulfilled the plan He had made for her. She diligently had seen to every last detail of the good work He had prepared beforehand for her to do. It was time for a new life to begin, one that would never end. He showed up, gathered my beloved into His arms, and took her home with Him.

We all still miss her presence in our life, which brings with it a measure of sadness. Matt had a very hard time when he lost her. For the next eight months, He walked with the Lord, seeking Him and trying to understand. He grew up in a ministry environment. He has ministered to many people for decades. You cannot be around Spirit-filled believers for long without seeing miracles happen. It was one of the joys of Matt's life to be able to see God answer prayers and heal people of a diverse number of things. Matt strongly believes in prayer, particularly since his faith had become sight so often.

He loved his mother and wasn't ready for her to leave. Over 30,000 people praying and believing for Brenda's healing added conviction to his faith. He never doubted that she would be healed. Matt became angry with God for several months when she died that day. The hard, unanswerable questions kept swirling in his soul. "Why" was at the beginning of each one of them.

God loved Matt through every step of this. He let him have his anger and never left his side. Then one night, Matt had a vivid dream of such clarity that he could still see every detail in his mind. In his dream, he saw Brenda. She was obviously in Heaven, a lush environment with green pastures and beautiful trees. As Matt approached her, she looked at him and said, "Matt, tell your dad how much I love him. Oh, and be sure to tell Jaime how proud I am of her."

He assured her he would do those things as he walked toward her. Getting closer, he noticed a man standing not too far away. There were tears on his mother's face as she looked at Matt and explained she had to make a very hard decision. Matt could tell she was upset about whatever it was. He tried to lighten the conversation and said, "Mom, do you get to ride motorcycles up here?" Before she could answer, the man spoke up and said, "Yes, we ride them all the time." Matt then turned back to speak to Brenda, but she was gone. When he looked back at the man, he was also gone. It was then that he woke up.

Later, when he was praying about the dream, he was sure it was an important message God had sent him. As he and his wife Jaime talked about it, she reminded him about the medical updates they had gotten about Brenda as the disease progressed.

"Matt, her organs had all been severely damaged. If she had lived, she would not have been able to regain the life she loved living. God prompted you to ask about the motorcycles so you could understand she wouldn't be able to do that here. She was an active, involved, capable person before she got sick. Do you think she would have wanted to stay on earth if she couldn't live like that anymore?"

Matt said he immediately knew and understood this was what her hard decision was about. To stay on earth in a broken body or to go home with Jesus were the options that had been offered to her. We all knew the magnitude of her love for everybody on her path. We knew it was just as hard for her to leave as it was for us to let her go. However, we never doubted that she would rather be with Jesus than be here and feel like she was a burden to everyone rather than a blessing.

Paul wrote to the Philippians about a similar situation in his life. It is recorded in the first chapter beginning in verse nineteen. *"For I know that as you pray for me and the Spirit of Jesus Christ helps me, this will lead to my deliverance. For I fully expect and hope that I will never be ashamed, but that I will continue to be bold for Christ, as I have been in the past. And I trust that my life will bring honor to Christ, whether I live or die. For to me, living means living for Christ, and dying is even better. But if I live, I can do more fruitful work for Christ. So, I really don't know which is better. I'm torn between two desires: I long to go and be with Christ, which would be far better for me. But for your sakes, it is better that I continue to live."* Because of the ravaged condition of her body, when Brenda was faced with the same option, it was far better for her to go to be with Him.

That foul evil, COVID-19, didn't take my precious wife. Nor was it able to kill her. It is impossible to kill a Christian – you can only move them home sooner. In Second Corinthians, the Scriptures are clear, *"We are confident, yes, well pleased rather to be absent from the body and to be present with the Lord."* You can't kill a Christian because they immediately enter the Lord's presence and finally live life fully.

One day, each of us will come to the moment when it is time for the Lord to show up. When my time comes, I'm not going to heaven to look for Brenda first. There will be streets of gold, gates made of a single pearl, and all the wonders we find described in the Scriptures. However, I'm not going because of the things that He has prepared for us in heaven. I'm going so that I can see face to face the One who gave Himself for me so He could then give Himself to me. Honestly, I can't wait to be present with the Lord.

Once I am with Him, I will search for my beloved, Brenda. What a glorious moment that will be. I will finally fulfill the promise I made to her so many years ago as we stood at the departure gate at Love Field.

When I'm in heaven, I'll meet her at the arrival gate at the Source of Pure Love. No longer will I be disfigured; because I will have been transfigured into my glorified body. At last, I will have returned home to Brenda without a scar.

THE END

APPENDIX I

APPENDIX II

Dave Roever is the founder and president of three non-profit corporations ministering in seventy countries worldwide. They are Roever Evangelistic Association, REAP International, and Roever Foundation, all based in Fort Worth, Texas. He also is the founder of Eagles Summit Ranch in Colorado and Eagles Summit Ranch in Texas, where he helps physically and emotionally injured servicemen and women "find their way home." There is a summary of each of the three organizations below; however, you will find additional information on their website, which can be quickly accessed by scanning their QR code.

Roever Evangelistic Association — www.daveroever.org

Dave Roever grew up in a minister's family in South Texas. At the height of the Vietnam War, Dave received his draft notice. Rather than serving in the infantry, he joined the U.S. Navy and served as a riverboat gunner in the elite Brown Water Black Beret in Vietnam.

Eight months into his tour of duty in Vietnam, Roever was burned beyond recognition when a phosphorous grenade he was poised to throw exploded in his hand. The ordeal left him hospitalized for fourteen months, where he underwent numerous major surgeries. His survival and life are miraculous.

Today with his humorous style, Roever is enthusiastically received both nationally and internationally as a public speaker. He is a superb communicator and speaks in a variety of settings including churches, public schools; business, men's and youth conventions; and military installations around the world. Roever has also been a frequent guest on national television talk shows. He established compassionate, ongoing missions work in Vietnam and is involved in other nations.

REAP International – www.reapworldwide.com

Roever Educational Assistance Programs (REAP) International is the educational arm of Roever & Associates. REAP has partnered with Global University a non-profit Christian university. Together we have developed an online Christian discipleship and ministry training program. This program provides spiritual discipleship for effective ministry. We offer online discipleship and ministry training to everyone in the world.

Roever Foundation – www.roeverfoundation.org

The Roever Foundation has a long and exciting history in support of public education, the US military, assistance to servicemen and women, and tours in military war zones.

Military ~ With public speaking opportunities engaging the troops with a message of hope, Roever Foundation has reached across the globe. From military installations stateside to troops stationed in peace-keeping efforts abroad and downrange in the height of war, we have encouraged those serving America to be resilient and stand strong.

Operation Warrior RECONnect (OWR) ~ Our military influence goes one step further. Roever Foundation has developed Operation Warrior RECONnect, a division that offers various programs for military, first responders, their spouses, and families to attend. These programs all contribute to the emotional health of our service members and their entire family.

Schools ~ The Roever Foundation has supported the efforts in public school assemblies in a like manner as military tours with inspirational speaking to over seven million students in over thirty years. Students are challenged to live with solid, moral character when faced with life's difficulties. The examples given by the Roever Foundation speakers through their personal life stories prove that it is possible to overcome adversity.

Other Outreaches of Roever Foundation ~ Roever Foundation is honored to share at corporate events, business meetings, national conventions, city and state functions and various community outreaches. Sharing hope and encouragement with people is our DNA. Leaving a community better than we found it is our goal.

About Stan Corvin, Jr.

Born in a small town in West Texas during WWII, Stan grew up in a military family. His father, a career U.S. Air Force fighter pilot from 1939 to 1974, retired as a colonel, and his mother was an elementary school teacher. After attending Texas Tech University, Stan was drafted into the U.S. Army in 1967 and was accepted into helicopter flight school during basic training, graduating nine months later. He flew helicopters in Vietnam from 1968-69 as a "loach" pilot for a "hunter-killer" team and then as a covert operations pilot for the CIA from 1971-72. Attaining the rank of captain, Stan resigned his U.S. Army commission in 1974.

After working forty years in banking and commercial lending, Stan retired, then wrote and published *"Vietnam Saga: Exploits of a Combat Helicopter Pilot."* On August 27, 2022, it was awarded a silver medal by the Military Writers Society of America. A riveting personal memoir about his three years of flying during the Vietnam War tells of him being shot down twice in ten minutes at Khe Sanh on April 29, 1972. He was trying to save a lone American fighter pilot who had bailed out and was surrounded by 12,500 NVA soldiers. After being shot four times in the chest and stomach by an enemy AK-47, Stan and his crewmembers were pinned down in a muddy rice paddy for thirteen hours before being rescued!

Other books written by Stan Corvin, Jr.:

"Echoes of the Hunt, A Texan Told True Tall."

(2019 1ˢᵗ place winner Texas Authors Association.)

"The Eagle Above: Chronicles of an American Fighter Pilot."

As Co-author:

"Jet Pioneer: A Fighter Pilot's Memoir."

"Vietnam Abyss: A Journal of Unmerited Grace."

"Attacked at Home: A Green Beret's Survival Story of the Fort Hood Shooting."

Other Southwestern Legacy Press Books:

"Skibirds: Adventures of the Raven Gang."

"It's Your Eternity: Last Breath, Then What?"

"I Volunteered for This: A Woman's Perspective of Serving In the U.S. Army."

"Diamond in the Darkness: Abused Child of Darkness, Reclaimed Daughter of Light."

Available in Amazon Books, Kindle, Barnes & Noble,
Audible.com, and iTunes.

Made in the USA
Monee, IL
08 May 2023

33239675R10096